HOW
TO SAVE
MORE
MONEY

More money at the end of the month

With simple magic lifehacks in your own kitchen

What you have to do to have more money at the end of the month via a win-win situation!

Save up to € 270 electricity per year when buying new kitchen appliances.

If you use also the saving tips, you can save up to € 100 year per year.

Up to 370 € every year more money in your purse!

ONLY WITH YOUR OWN KITCHEN!

WHETHER IN YOUR OWN HOME OR IN YOUR RENTED HOME!
IT WORKS EVERYWHERE!

From

Master Physicist & Master Engineer

Alexander Goldmann

Translated from the original version from German

Second revised edition

Preface

Congratulations!

The first step for more money at the end of the month.

You only have to live consciously in your own apartment. The tips and hints presented here will help you to achieve exactly this promise.

Without taking risks, without building a business, without having to invest much or without investing with any money at all. It's the easiest way to "make money".

And all of this with indulgence and comfort!

I have deliberately kept myself short so that you always have the most important information at a glance. Therefore, you will also find tables with which you can quickly decide to find exactly the specific electrical appliance that suits you and at the same time saves you money.

In addition, you can see at a glance, with which very simple steps you can get more money for your current device for yourself.

Read the book to the end you will find some bonuses, which will help you more easily to achieve your goals!

Keep more of your hard-earned money!

With this I wish you much fun and interest with this book!

TIP: At the end of the book there are some bonuses for you! Don't miss it!

Table of content

PREFACE...4

TABLE OF CONTENT...6

MOTIVATION 9

SAVING IS THE BETTER YIELD.............................12

INTRODUCTION..14

INTRODUCTION TO UNITS AND FORMULAS OF
CALCULATIONS..16

THE FRIDGE 18

POSSIBILITIES AND SUPPORT FOR YOUR DECISION-MAKING: THE
FRIDGE...18
SAVING TIPS FOR THE FRIDGE...............................25
FRIDGE – HOW IT WORKS......................................34
ENERGY LABEL FRIDGE..36

THE DISHWASHER 46

POSSIBILITIES AND SUPPORT FOR YOUR DECISION-MAKING: THE
DISHWASHER...47
SAVING TIPS DISHWASHER 55
WORK PRINCIPLE DISHWASHER............................61
ENERGY LABEL DISHWASHER 64

THE OVEN 67

POSSIBILITIES AND SUPPORT FOR YOUR DECISION MAKING – THE OVEN 67

FUNCTION PRINCIPLE OVEN 84

ENERGY LABEL – OVEN 86

POSSIBILITIES & SUPPORT FOR YOUR DECISION-MAKING 91

SAVING TIPS STOVEN 96

FUNCTION-PRINCIPLE STOVE 100

ENERGY LABEL FOR THE STOVE - NOT AVAILABLE 101

THE MICROWAVE 102

DECISION-MAKING POSSIBILITIES & SUPPORT FOUR YOUR DECISION MAKING – THE MICROWAVE 104

SAVING TIPS FOR THE MICROWAVE 107

FUNCTION PRINCIPLE – THE MICROWAVE 112

ENERGY LABEL MICROWAVE - NOT AVAILABLE 114

THE KETTLE 115

DECISION-MAKING POSSIBILITIES & SUPPORT FOR YOUR DECISION-MAKING FOR THE KETTLE 117

SAVING TIPS FOR THE KETTLE 120

FUNCTION PRINCIPLE FOR THE KETTLE 124

ENERGY LABEL FOR THE ELECTRIC KETTLE - NOT AVAILABLE 125

THE TOASTER 126

DECISION-MAKING POSSIBILITIES & SUPPORT FOR YOUR DECISION-MAKING – THE TOASTER 128

SAVING TIPS TOASTER 133

ENERGY LABEL TOASTER - NOT AVAILABLE 134

DECISION-MAKING POSSIBILITIES & SUPPORT FOR YOUR DECISION-MAKING 144

THE WALL BOX 151

THE WATER HEATER 160

OPERATION PRINCIPLE OF THE WATER HEATER 160

COMPARISON WITH OTHER SYSTEMS 163

FUNCTIONAL PRINCIPLE OF A FULLY ELECTRONIC INSTANTANEOUS WATER HEATERS 167

DECISION-MAKING OPPORTUNITIES AND SUMMARY FOR THE INSTANTANEOUS WATER HEATER 170

SAVING TIPS INSTANTANEOUS WATER HEATER 180

ENERGY LABEL WATER HEATER 183

THE STAND-BY OPERATION 189

THE FUTURE OF THE KITCHEN 193

WHAT IS ENERGY EFFICIENCY? 210

WHAT IS AN ENERGY EFFICIENCY TABLE / ENERGY LABEL? 210

WHAT IS ELECTRICITY / ELECTRICAL CURRENT? 211

WHAT IS A MAGNETIC FIELD? 211

EPILOGUE 213

BONUS PAGES 215

AWESOME BEGINNER CHECKLIST TO SAVE MONEY QUICKLY 216

LIST OF FIGURES 220

LIST OF TABLES 222

IMPRINT..**225**

BIBLIOGRAPHY..**226**

Motivation

You live in a household, am I right? Every household has a kitchen and in 99% of all households exists a fridge. And most households have next to the refrigerator other household appliances, such as an oven, microwave, etc. This is the reason why I want to help you in this book with the help of your own kitchen to save unnecessarily spent money, so your hard earned money stays in your wallet and you do not have to waste it senselessly.

In addition, I want to clean up with some representations. For example, on the internet some insane bills in which an oven is used for one hour a day and is said to incur with an average cost of almost € 200 a year.

Conscious budgeting not only keeps more money in your account, but also helps to protect the environment by reducing CO_2 emissions. This is a win-win situation that everyone wants.

In recent years, electricity prices have risen sharply, as you have certainly seen even on your own electricity bill. In Figure 1 you can see the electricity prices in Europe in cents per kilowatt-hour (kWh) divided into countries with the share of taxes and duties. Compared to the European Union (EU) with an average cost of 20.4 cents / kWh, the Germans pay the most for electricity with the long-standing leader Denmark with 30.5 cents / kWh. Compared to the neighbors Czech Republic (14.4 cents / kWh) and Poland (14.6 cents / kWh), people in Germany pay twice as much. In the last ten years from 2007 to 2017 alone, electricity prices have risen by 39%.

But what can you do about it?

Well, you can wait and hope that the government does something about it or the energy companies are so nice and will meet your concerns. If you ask me, that will unlikely happen. Or you can take it into your own hands and try to reduce your energy consumption without any effort.

And as I like to say:

"SAVING IS THE BETTER YIELD"

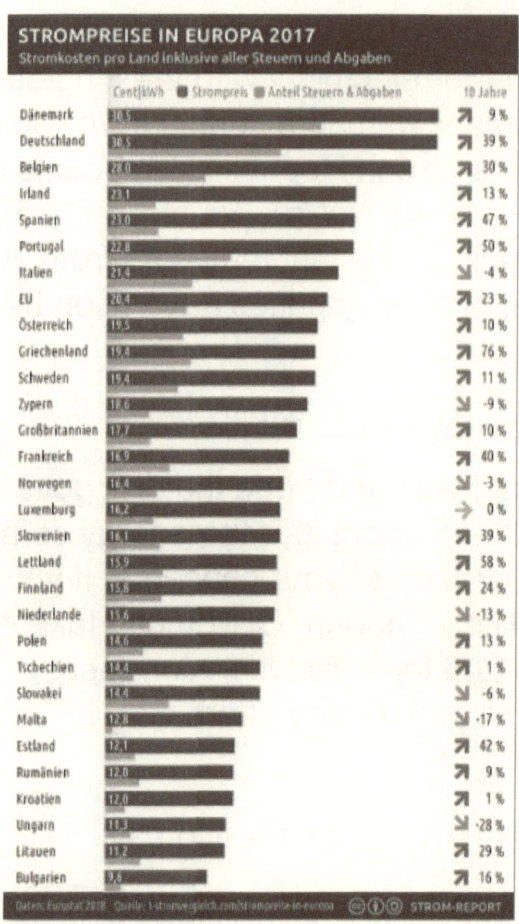

Figure 1: Overview of electricity prices in Europe in cents per kWh, including the share of taxes and duties.[1]

1   [1] (https://1-stromvergleich.com, 2018)

Saving is the better yield

Why do I claim that you get a better return of yield when you save money rather than investing money?

Let's say you own $ 10,000 and you want to invest them. A small fortune, right?

If you invest them for 1% a year, and you need to take some time to find a place where you get these interest, then you get after a year 100 € interest. That's not bad, but you have to have 10.000 € for this. Your return is 1% (before taxes).

Now let's take one of the examples in this book that you will find here. If you turn off the oven 15 minutes before the end, rather than using it for your pizza or cake until the very end, you would not have to heat for 15 minutes, right? You can do this without worry, because the heat lasts for about 15 minutes in the oven the same and you would see no difference in the result. Assuming the average electricity cost of 30.5 cents / kWh and an average oven output of 3000 kWh, you would save about 23 cents per baking course. Now suppose you use the oven once a week, 52 times a year, you would have saved about 12 € a year. Only with turning off the oven 15 minutes before the end of baking.

Or in other words. You've "created" $ 1200 on your bank account. Because this sum you would need at 1% interest to get 12 € interest a year.

Since you have not invested any money, you theoretically have a return of "infinite". Not bad, right?

What I want to say with this is, that you would need a lot of money on your account to get the same return as if you were saving or reducing your power consumption.

Rational and useful, isn't it?

Then go ahead and continue with the book.

Introduction

Almost all households, 99.9%, have a refrigerator in Germany.

What for a huge saving potential for Germany. So do you! If every household would only use energy saving tips for the fridge, the benefit potential is huge. I explain this to you with a theoretical example.

In 2016 in Germany there were 40.9 million private households. Accordingly, there are just as many refrigerators. Let's assume that 10% of all households own a refrigerator which is 15 years or older. If these 10% would convert this into a new A + refrigerator (not an A+++), this would save about 1 billion kilowatt hours (kWh) of electricity per year. That's a whole terawatt hour (TWh). This allows an 18 watt energy-saving lamp to shine continuously over 6300 years. Or you could go around the globe eleven times with a Tesla Roadster. Each year.

At a current average electricity price of 30.5 cents per kWh, the electricity bill for a household for its own refrigerator would be reduced by approximately € 57. And this year after year. If the electricity price increases, which is not so unlikely, your savings will increase again. So, this is roughly equivalent to a salary increase, right? Only that you would get this salary increase with each electricity price increase.

Let run this example through your head.

Introduction to units and formulas of calculations

Electrical appliances require energy, which we usually provide with electrical energy. A LED lamp needs a certain amount of power to light up. This power is expressed in watts, in short "W". 1000 watts is equal to 1 kilowatt (kW). How much you have to pay to your municipal utilities is calculated how much work is done, which power is needed in which time.

If a LED lamp requires 20 watts and burns for 10 hours, it has a work of 20 W x 10 hours (h) = 200 Wh = 0.2 kWh. The average electricity price is 30.5 cents per kWh. You would have to pay 0.3 kWh x 0.305 € = 0.0915 € = 9.15 cents for the 10 hours.

To keep it simple for now, we claim that this lamp burns every day for a year 10 hours a day. Whether this makes sense or not, we will talk later about it.

The year has 365 days, that means 0,0915 € x 365 = 33,40 €.

Let a 20 W lamp burn for 10 hours every day and you pay around 33 € a year. Only for the lamp? Right, 33 € for a single lamp. There are also other electrical appliances such as oven, stove, electric kettle, washing machine, hair drier, etc. A household can theoretically have up to 100 electrical appliances and each of them requires electricity for it. Probably you own about 30 electrical appliances at home. You can count them if you like. A list of possible electrical appliances can be found on page 207. This is how your electricity bill is calculated. And now, we will reduce your electricity bill.

Let's start with the fridge.

The fridge

Possibilities and Support for your decision-making: The Fridge

Saving up to 100 € with new purchases and additional to this with simple practical tips xtra 20 € every single year, only with a single household appliance, the refrigerator? Is this possible?

It is possible!

30% of Germans worry about their future pension. The money is tight and every penny has to be counted. Why should you pay too much money for the electricity of the household appliances?

When people were still hunters and gatherers, cooling food was not a big issue. They consumed everything in time. When the first primitive agriculture began about 12,000 years ago, people settled down and lived in one place. To cool the food, people became inventive. They dug holes in the ground or used the cooling river. In the middle ages, the slightly cooler niches in the wooden walls were used. Later, the cellar was often used and with the help of wooden barrels and clay pots perishable foods were made more durable. For this purpose, ice was even taken from the mountains and used in the cellars for cooling. This basically corresponds to the principle of a refrigerator, although if you say "cooling room", it would be more accurate.

The Scot William Cullen developed in 1748 the first artificial cooling. However, this was used for room cooling for hospital patients. Further developments took until 1834 until the first refrigerators were commercialized. It can be said that from the 1930s on the fridge became standard in the households.

But the development of the refrigerator continued. In addition to cooling, there are many more options and features today.

You should know these options and features in order to make the most fundamental decision possible for you.

When buying a new refrigerator, you should first of all determine the design. Should the refrigerator stand free in the room or should it be a built-in appliance? For an efficient machine, you should energetically refer to the freestanding refrigerator. Here, the air outside the unit can circulate better and supports the extraction of the heat. The refrigerator works more efficiently. And if it works more efficiently, it needs less energy respectively electricity. And that's exactly what we want to achieve.

With the product type you decide for yourself what you need. A full-size refrigerator which only cools, a freezer which just freezes or a fridge-freezer which can do both in a single unit. The last one is a practical way to both cool and freeze in a relatively small space. A two-door refrigerator in which the doors are attached to the side, also called side-by-side, looks visually good, but requires a lot of space. Due to the more space and the size, the energy consumption is higher. The French Door Refrigerator is similar to the side-by-side refrigerator. This fridge also has the two big doors. The main difference here is the higher number of doors, such as one or two drawers, which serve as a freezer. These drawers can be mounted, for example, below the refrigerator and looks similar to a cabinet. The pros and cons are the same as the side-by-side refrigerator.

For the net capacity, you can use the following rule of thumb. The first person requires 100 liters capacity, for each additional person add 50 liters. For a 2-person household, the rule of thumb would say 100 liters + 50 liters = 150 liters.

What here counts to save money is, it should be as small as possible and as big as necessary!

Everyone has a different food consumption behavior and different rituals, that's why the perfect customized refrigerator is always individual. Watch yourself a few days or weeks. Do you really need the largest refrigerator in which you could even lock yourself up? Maybe for the hot summer it is not so a strange idea. For the energy consumption, however, an idea that I would not suggest.

For the energy efficiency class, make sure that you have selected at least a device with A+. Who wants to have an inefficient machine at home and paying too much electricity unnecessarily every single month?

Do not ignore the noise level. If your fridge is louder than your conversation partner, that does not add much to the mood and you may have picked the wrong refrigerator. A refrigerator under 40 dB is considered as quiet. You should also note that only the hum of a refrigerator can cause you sleepless nights or at least problems while sleeping with as little as 30 decibels[2]. Do not save money when it causes health problems!

A fridge-freezer with about 120 liters capacity and an energy class A++ is already available from about 300 €. If you would replace a 15-year-old refrigerator with

---

2   [5] (Esche, 2016)

an A+ refrigerator, you can save about € 100 a year. After just 3 years, you would earn € 100 every single year. This would correspond to a virtual assets of € 10,000, as explained at the beginning, with 1% interest.

Below you can find an overview of all options and their potential savings for you. The words written in bold should be preferred in terms of energy.

Fridge	
Possibilities for your decisions	**Help for your decisions**
Design	Built-in appliances Free in the room appliances
Product type	Big fridge Fridge-freezer combination (most common type) Side-by-Side French Door Freezer
Net capacity	Individually. As a rule of thumb: 100 liters for the first person, for each additional person 50 liters. What here counts is: "As small as possible and as big as necessary."
Energy efficiency	From energy class G to A+++ possible (It should have at least an A+).

Volume	Below 40 dB is quiet
Annual electricity consumption	With 100 liters net capacity under 100 kWh are very good.
Acquisition cost	100 liters of net capacity from about 200 € available. To over 2000 € possible.
Savings potential with new purchase	100 € per year.

Table 1: Possibilities and help for your decisions for the fridge.

Saving tips for the fridge

There are a handful of tips that you just have to do once and then benefit from it all the time. This cannot be compared to an employee job where you trade your time for money. With a single tiny handgrip of say 10 minutes in a single day, you can save money every single month. This is what you should aim for. Doing a job once and benefit from it all your lifetime.

One example is, that it plays a crucial role where and how the refrigerator stands so that it can work efficiently. For example, it should not be inside a cabinet, because there the heat can not be removed. This reduces efficiency, whereby this increases your electricity bill.

Keep at least five cm space at the back of the wall to allow the heat to escape easily. As a result, the heat of the coolant can be removed better. On the back side there is also a grid and the cooling tube. These should be dust free. The dust acts as an insulation and therefore the heat can be removed worse,which makes the refrigerator more inefficient.

The refrigerator should be away from heat sources, such as heaters or stoves and should be protected from direct sunlight. Otherwise, the device would heat up unnecessarily and you have to pay for its cooling.

Keep the ambient temperature as cool as possible. Lowering the ambient temperature from 21 degrees to 20 degrees results in a power saving of 6% [3]. Therefore, the coolest rooms in the apartment are the most suitable ones, which is often the kitchen itself or a storage room. If you have a cellar, this would be the best place to park. However, you would have to go to the basement each time you want to get something from the bridge. For the one who wants to lose weight, that's no problem, for everyone else it can be a challenge. Therefore, it is important to balance between cost savings and comfort.

The seals of the refrigerator should be well sealed and non-porous so that the cold stays inside the refrigerator, where it belongs. I do not think you really want to cool your kitchen with the fridge. However this would not be possible, because the heat you just made cold, is transported to the back of the fridge, which is still in the kitchen. As a test, you can put a flashlight in the fridge, close the door and see from outside if light shines through. If you see the light, it is a sign that the renewal of the seal should be considered.

---

3   [6] (Meyer, 2018)

The higher the ice layer inside the device, the higher the energy consumption. Therefore, it should be defrosted regularly. It would be most convenient to buy the anti-frost function when buying new ones. This saves time but also costs money. Because the refrigerator is heated for a short time, so that the ice melts and thus can drain as water. After that, of course, the interior must be cooled down again.

Open the door of the refrigerator as less as possible. According to Co2online, the energy consumption of a short opening of the refrigerator corresponds to the ten-minute consumption of a 60 watt light bulb. This means a ten-time opening costs you about 3 cents. If you opened the door ten times every day all year, you would have to pay € 11 more in electricity each year. This should be considered as an example. You know best how often you open the refrigerator door.

Adjust the cooling of your refrigerator as low as possible and as high as necessary. You can save about 6% of energy per degree Celsius[4]. It is understood that this can not be done linearly and this should only be seen as a rule of thumb.
Nevertheless, you can see here how easily electricity can be saved. The optimum temperature is generally 7 degrees and -18 degrees in the freezer.

---

4   [7] (Verbraucherzentrale, 2016)

Place the food which need the most cooling at the bottom and the food that can be warmer at the top of the refrigerator. Since a certain temperature gradient exists within the refrigerator, this can be used. However this is no longer the case in a fridge with a circulating air function.

Within the refrigerator you should order so that the air can circulate. For refrigerators without air circulation function, the temperature gradient can be several degrees Celsius. Keeping the fridge full will allow less air to escape when you open the door. Thus, the device must cool down less. Nevertheless, 20-30% of the refrigerator should remain free to maintain the circulation of the air and thus allows the cold air to reach all the food.

Allow warm food to cool down before putting it back in the refrigerator. When the food reaches room temperature, put it in. Why should the refrigerator do this work if you can do it for free?

After purchasing cooled down or frozen goods in the supermarket, you should bring them to your refrigerator as soon as possible and by the shortest route. It is best to use cool bags or coolers along the way. The colder the food is, the less the appliance has to cool it down and you save money.

In winter, you can have your drinks and food outside cooled by nature for free and then put them in the fridge. If it has about 7 degrees Celsius in the open air, this corresponds to the refrigerator temperature. You can use it. When I moved to another city I didn't have yet a fridge, so I had to put my food and beverages anyway to my balcony. I was lucky, it was winter and the temperatur in this period was about 5-8 degrees. It worked just fine. Just make sure that the food is well sealed.

→ If you think about this tip, you could even cool the fridge itself, not the other way around. Wouldn't this be amazing? For this purpose, a ventilation system would have to be led from outside to inside to the refrigerator. This should be a closed system for reasons of hygiene. Unfortunately, during my research, I could not find a refrigerator that has this or a similar function or is constructed in this way. Especially in winter, the compressor would almost no longer work, as the average temperature in winter 2017/2018 in Germany was 1.6 degrees Celsius[5].

It is recommended to replace your old device with a new one after 10-15 years at the latest, because there have been many developments during this

---

5   [8] (Statista, 2018)

period. But please note here that you should think twice about keeping and using the old fridge. Because then you have two refrigerators that you have to pay for. It's best to just keep the new efficient refrigerator and try to recycle or sell the old one if possible.

Fridge	
Saving possibilities	**Help for you decision making**
Location	Keep distance from heat sources.

Do not put in a cabinet.

Keep at least 5 cm behind to the wall.

If the ambient temperature is lowered from 21 to 20 degrees, this results in a power saving of about **6%**. |
| Door openings | Open the door as less and as quick as possible. 10 times door openings costs you about 3 cents. |
| Air circulation | Remove the dust at the rear and the cooling tube.

For appliances in cabinets, remove dust from the ventilation slots. |
| Order / packing density | Inside there should be as much order as possible, so |

	that the air can circulate. Keep the refrigerator full so that less air can escape when opening the door. Nevertheless, 20-30% of the refrigerator should remain free (circulation).
Seals	Check seals for leaks.
Avoid icing inside	Defrost regularly.
Turn cooling down	Per degree Celsius of higher set temperature saves you approx. 5% of energy.
Let warm food cool down first	Even better: at cold weather, let the food cool down on the balcony.
Transport	Transport purchased cooled down goods to home with cool bags.
Potential savings per year	Approximately 20 € saving potential per year.
New device	Exchange of old device after 10-15 years recommended.

Table 2: Savings options and help for your decision-makings for the refrigerator

Fridge – How it works

The principle of the refrigerator is the same principle as it is used in air conditioners. Those who understand it can explain most of the cooling principles in the world. So pay attention!

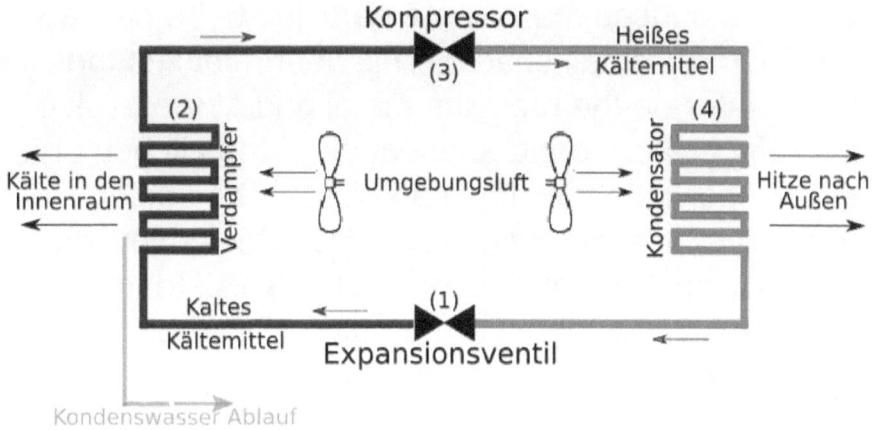

Figure 2: Basic principle of the functioning of a refrigerator.

The refrigerator uses the reverse principle of the second law of thermodynamics: heat flows towards the cold. So if you do not intervene, heat always flows in the direction of the cold. But now we do the reverse: coldness should flow in the direction of heat. Since this does not happen by itself we need energy, in this case electricity - for which you pay. A refrigerator works by evaporating and re-liquefying a "coolant", it has a boiling point of -30°C (water has a boiling point of 100°C). When evaporating in the expansion valve (1), the refrigerant becomes cold and can absorb heat from the coolant (2) - this makes the refrigerator cool. The vapour absorbs this heat and is led to the outside of the refrigerator, where the coolant liquefies with pressure in the compressor (3), thereby becoming even hotter (the pressure causes many more particles to be packed together in a small space). This heat releases the refrigerator on the rear (the metal grid at the back of the refrigerator) to the ambient air of the kitchen and the refrigerant cools down again (4). The cooled refrigerant is again evaporated (1), which makes it naturally colder (physical principle). This steam can resume the heat of the refrigerator. This process is simply repeated over and over again.

Basically, the gas is repeatedly expanded and compressed and by taking advantage of this physical principle, the interior of the refrigerator is cooled.

The condensation produced by this process is collected at the back of the unit, where it is evaporated.

Energy Label Fridge

How efficiently a device can convert or consume electricity has been indicated in Europe since 1996 with an energy label or also called EU label. The consumer should be able to see at one glance how economical a device is and make it easier to compare devices when buying new ones. The energy label contains only pictograms and is therefore language neutral. The classes are marked with the letters A to G with colors. Due to advances in technology, the classes have now been extended with A+, A++ and A+++. Since this has suffered for the clarity of the labels and there are different classes for each device (there are only A-classes available for washing machines), it was decided in 2017 to make the labels uniform again. From 2020, only the designations A-G will be visible again. The A's with the "+" characters will therefore be omitted.

An energy label must be available for the following household appliances:

- Refrigerators and freezers
- Dishwasher
- Washing machine
- Clothes dryer

- Electric oven and gas oven

- Hoods

- Vacuum cleaner

- TV

- Lamps

- Heaters

- Boiler

- Solid fuel boiler

- Composite systems

- Single room heaters

- Air conditioning

- Indoor ventilation equipment

In figure 3 you can see the current energy efficiency classes of the just listed devices. The colored bars indicate which energy classes are currently available. The dashed lines indicate which energy classes will be discontinued in the near future or have already been eliminated.

It should be noted that the merchants themselves determine the class. There is no independent institute that controls this. For spot checks, the consumer advice center has already identified deficiencies. In the washing machine, for example, the manufacturers choose only the eco or savings program and define with this the whole device.

From 2019, the EU wants to make an online database available to the public in which consumers can compare the devices more easily. But until this was written nothing was published by the EU.

Figure 4 shows the energy labeling for refrigerators and freezers. Here you can find the brand or the name of the manufacturer with model name (1), the energy efficiency class (2), the energy consumption in kilowatt hours (kWh) per year (3). In addition, you can see at a glance the total net capacity of all refrigerators in liters (4), the total net capacity of all freezers in liters (5) and the volume in decibels (dB) (6).

For the refrigerator the best energy efficiency is currently class A +++. The classes A to D are currently no longer available. From 2020 on, all energy labels will be standardized again to classes A to G.

Energielabel: Aktuelle Energieeffizienzklassen nach Produktgruppen (Teil 1)

Auf dem Energielabel sind meist sieben Energieeffizienzklassen[1] dargestellt. Die beste Klasse variiert zwischen A und A+++, je nach Produktgruppe. Bei Haushaltsgeräten sind viele Klassen für Neugeräte gar nicht mehr zugelassen! Da sie die Mindestanforderungen der europäischen Ökodesign-Verordnungen nicht erfüllen, dürfen sie nicht mehr in den Verkehr gebracht werden. Diese Klassen sind grau schraffiert dargestellt.

Stand: Januar 2018

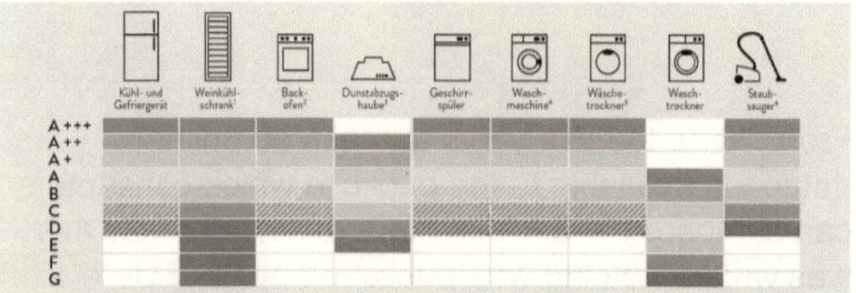

[1] Ausnahme Weinkühlschrank: Das Energielabel umfasst 10 Klassen.
[2] Ein Teil der Klasse B darf bereits seit 20. Februar 2016 nicht mehr in den Verkehr gebracht werden, 2019 fällt die gesamte Klasse B weg und ein Teil von A.
[3] Energielabel mit Klassen A+++ bis D darf bereits verwendet werden (Pflicht ab 2020).
[4] Mit mehr als 4 kg Beladekapazität.
[5] Bei Ablufttrocknern ist Klasse C noch erlaubt.
[6] Leistungsaufnahme darf max. 900 W betragen.

© HEA 2018

Energielabel: Aktuelle Energieeffizienzklassen nach Produktgruppen (Teil 2)

Produkte werden auf dem Energielabel meist in sieben Energieeffizienzklassen eingeteilt, es können aber bis zu zehn sein. Einige Klassen sind für Neugeräte nicht mehr zugelassen. Da sie die Mindestanforderungen der europäischen Ökodesign-Verordnungen nicht erfüllen, dürfen sie nicht mehr in den Verkehr gebracht werden. Diese Klassen sind grau schraffiert dargestellt.

Stand: Januar 2018

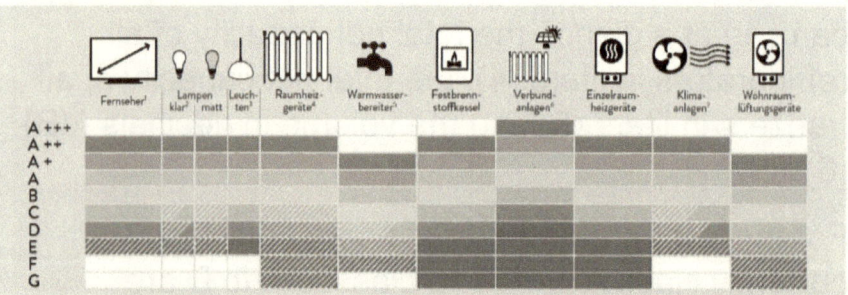

[1] Das Energielabel mit den Klassen A+++ bis D bereits verwendet werden.
[2] Ungerichtete Halogenlampen der Klassen C und D dürfen noch bis 31. August 2018 neu in den Verkehr gebracht werden. Danach fallen neben Glüh- auch Halogenlampen unter das Verkaufsverbot (bis auf wenige Ausnahmen).
[3] Können Lampen bestimmter Klassen nicht in einer Leuchte verwendet werden, müssen diese Klassen auf dem Label durchgestrichen werden.
[4] Bei Kombigeräten wird auf dem Label zusätzlich die Warmwasserbereitung mit den Klassen A+ bis F gekennzeichnet. Die Ökodesign-Mindestanforderungen variieren je nach Beheizung.
[5] Die Ökodesign-Mindestanforderungen variieren je nach Lastprofil.
[6] Verbundanlagen aus einem Raumheizgerät bzw. Festbrennstoffkessel, Zusatzheizgeräten, Temperaturreglern und Solareinrichtungen.
[7] Geräte für das Kühlen und/oder Heizen von Innenraumluft. Die Ökodesign-Mindestanforderungen variieren je nach Funktion.

© HEA 2018

Figure 3: Current energy efficiency classes by product group. As of January 2018. Thanks goes to HEA. [9] (Conradi, 2018).

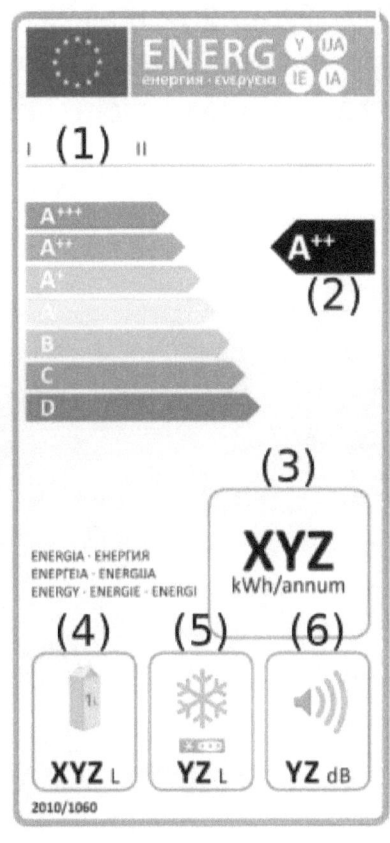

1) Tradename or name of the manufacturer with model name

2) Energy efficiency class

3) Energy consumption in kilowatt hours (kWh) per year
(Attention: How often the fridge is opened and how warm the food is, is not put into account and is not included here.)

4) Total net capacity of all refrigerators in liters

5) Total net capacity of all freezers in liters

6) Volume in decibels (dB)

Note on refrigerators and freezers:

The best energy efficiency class is A+++. The classes A to D are currently no longer

	available. From 2020, all energy labels will be standardized again to classes A to G.
Figure 4: Energy labeling for refrigerators and freezers.	

Calculation of energy efficiency classes

Below is a brief explanation of how the energy efficiency classes are calculated and classified. It should be mentioned here that the use of the devices, such as the number of opening the refrigerator or the oven door is not included. This is done to achieve standardization. Therefore, the individual consumption is always different. However, in my opinion, this should be included in the future calculation to ensure a more accurate consumption values.

The energy efficiency class is determined on the basis of the Energy Efficiency Index, EEI. Table 3 shows this classification as valid since 1st of July 2014.

Energy efficiency class	Energy efficiency index (EEI)
A+++ (highest efficiency)	EEI < 22
A++	22 ≤ EEI < 33
A+	33 ≤ EEI < 42
A	42 ≤ EEI < 55
B	55 ≤ EEI < 75

C	75 ≤ EEI < 95
D	95 ≤ EEI < 110
E	110 ≤ EEI < 125
F	125 ≤ EEI <150
G (lowest efficiency)	EEI ≥ 150

Table 3: Classification of the energy efficiency class by the Energy Efficiency Index (EEI).

The calculation of the Energy Efficiency Index (EEI) takes into account the energy consumption, the effective volume of the different storage compartments, the temperature of the storage compartments and a correction factor. This is measured in a laboratory to ensure standards such as the climate class. The climate classes are divided into extended temperate zone, temperate zone, subtropical zone and tropical zone.

If you are interested in the exact and complete calculation method, please refer to Annex VIII of the EU Regulation, as this would go deep into the detail: (*https://eur-ex.europa.eu/LexUriServ/LexUriServ.do?uri=OJ:L:2010:314:0017:0046:DE:PDF*).

Product data sheet

In addition to an energy label, each device must also be accompanied by a product data sheet. This information on the product data sheet must be presented in the following order with the corresponding units. Here is an example for the refrigerator.

- *Brand or name of the manufacturer*
- *Model identification*
- *Household refrigerating appliances categories*
- *Energy efficiency class*
- *Annual energy consumption in kWh per year*
- *Net capacity of each refrigerated compartment in liters and, if available, star marking*
- *Temperature other compartments*
- *Indication if frost free*
- *Storage time in case of fault in hours*
- *Freezing capacity in kilograms per 24 hours*
- *Climate class (Extended temperate zone (SN), Moderate zone (N), Subtropical zone (ST) and Tropical zone (T)*

- *Airborne noise emissions in decibels (dB)*
- *Specification of built-in device / integrate-able*
- *Specification wine storage cabinet*

The Dishwasher

The first dishwasher was developed in 1850 by Joel Houghton. Houghton couldn't sell very much, as people did not see the benefit for such a machine. They could buy a machine for a lot of money, while in contrast to that the own staff could make washing up the dishes a lot cheaper. Nowadays you want to avoid the more expensive staff with their many social benefits and use as many electrical appliances and machines as possible.

Times are changing.

In 1886, Josephine Cochrane signed up for a patent for the first mechanical dishwasher. In 1893 at the World's Fair in Chicago women were not allowed. That's why the first prize went to a so-called "Mr." Cochrane.

The dishwasher was brought to Europe by a tourist from Gütersloh, who told his father Reinhard Zinkann and his business partner Carl Miele the invention. They had long experience with electric motors, milk centrifuges and washing machines. Therefore, they already had experience and were interested in this new invention. In 1929, they patented the Model A, but it was so expensive that it was a really luxury item at this time. Due to the economic crisis and the two world wars, the dishwasher did not make it into the the German households. It was a long way for the device. First in 1960 the dishwasher with its typical flap started to generate decent sales. Since then, the device has been constantly developing and improving. In the last 20 years, the dishwasher's water consumption has been reduced by 70% and the electricity consumption by 50%.

Possibilities and Support for your decision-making: The Dishwasher

According to a study, you can use a dishwasher to save 50% of water and 28% of electricity compared to hand-washing[6]. The study was funded by household appliance and detergent manufacturers. It is up to you how much faith you want to give to this study.

If, in my opinion, the dishwasher is used properly, meaning, completely fully acknowledged and the eco-program is used, you can really save money with it. Because the dishwasher soaks the dishes and uses its water several times (see also page 65). If you compare that to a wasteful by-hand washer, who

---

6   [10] (www.br.de, 2017)

---

may always let run the water tap and has to rinse every single piece of cutlery at the end with clean water, then this study can at least point in the right direction.

If you want to buy a new dishwasher, you can lay the basis already with the new purchase to save up to 40 € per year.

You only need to consider the following possibilities.

There are a variety of variants with the design and you can decide what you need. If you order a new kitchen, you will probably decide for a base or built-in appliance. You can install a kitchen worktop for both. With the built-in appliance, you can also install a matching kitchen front in addition to your kitchen so that the dishwasher is optimally integrated into the kitchen. The stand unit can be placed freely in the room and has a fixed side panel and a sturdy removable top cover plate that you can use as an additional plate to put things on it. A modular dishwasher is a version of the built-in appliance that you can flexibly mount anywhere in the kitchen, for example at an ergonomic working height. The smallest variant is the table dishwasher. You can easily place it on the work table or any other surface. All you need is a power and a water connection.

The net capacity is divided up in the dishwasher in place settings. A place setting includes a dinner plate, a soup plate, a dessert plate, a cup with saucer, a glass and five pieces of cutlery. As a rule of thumb, a table dishwasher has room for about 5 place settings a dish washer with 45cm width about 9 place settings and one with 60cm width about 15 place settings. For a 3-person household a daily crockery of about 10 place settings is accumulated. This can be used as a starting point to calculate the appropriate size for your family. Not all people in the household and at work eat their meal at noon, so there are fewer place settings.

Tip: Often, the 60 cm wide dishwashers are more efficient than the other sizes, as this measure is sold the most and therefore is also primarily developed.

You should get at least one with an energy class A+. An appliance of efficiency class A+++ is about 15 percent more efficient than a dishwasher with A+. The water consumption should be between 8-10 liters per wash. If it is under 8 liters, this is considered as very good and very economical. An A+++ dishwasher consumes a maximum of 7 liters of water.

The noise level should be below 40 dB and is considered as quiet. A volume between 40-44 dB is considered as normal. For your own health, you should always pay attention to the volume of all the devices you buy and select the device whose noise levels you think are all right. Several studies show that noise makes you sick in the long term.

With the extras or equipments beside display and refill message much more is possible, therefore everyone has to decide this for themselves. However, attention should be paid to a program with a half load or an eco program. It can easily save water and electricity if the dishes are not overly dirty. Normally you can use an eco program is enough for all you dishes. You should sse this program.

With a new efficient dishwasher you save about 40 € electricity and water costs if you use the dishwasher five times per week compared to a device from 2002 on. A new dishwasher should at least have the efficiency class A +.

As a good overview of what was written, you are welcome to use the table below.

Dishwasher	
Possibilities for your decisions	**Help for your decisions**
Product type	Standing unit
	Appliance for cabinet
	Built-in device
	Modular dishwasher
	Tableware
Net capacity	Is divided into place settings.
	A set setting includes a dinner plate, a soup plate, a dessert plate, a cup with saucer, a glass and five pieces of cutlery.
	Rule of thumb:
	standing dishwasher 45cm width: about 9 place settings 60cm width: about 15 place settings Table-top dishwashers:

	approx. 5 place settings. 60cm wide dishwashers are usually more efficient as they are more common and most advanced.
Energy efficiency	From energy class A to A+++ (it should have at least a A+). A device with efficiency class A+++ is about 15% more efficient than a device with A+.
Water consumption	Per wash of 6 liters to 16 liters possible. Under 8 liters are very good. 8-10 liters should be maximum. A+++ devices consume max. 7 liters.
Volume	Below 40 dB is quiet. 40-44 dB are normal.
Equipment / Extras	In addition to display, refill display, etc. a lot is possible, therefore individual. Attention

	should be paid to a program with half load or eco program.
Number of programs	Individually, but an eco-program should be respected.
Latent- / heat storage	Some dishwashers use latent storage or heat storage to reuse the heat of the hot rinse water in another rinse. This can save up to 20% of electrical energy[7].
Annual electricity consumption	Approximately 200 kWh - 350 kWh written in the energy label, depending on size. A+++ to A: 30% more efficient A++ to A: 20% more efficient A+ to A: 10% more efficient

7   [27]

Acquisition cost	From about 200 € to over 3700 € possible.
Savings potential with new purchase	40 € saving potential per year.

Table 4: Possibilities and help for your decisions for the dishwasher.

Saving tips dishwasher

Depending on the program, the water for the dishwasher must also be heated. This is done by a normal heating wire, which does not make the dishwasher particularly efficient. You would benefit if you connect the hot water connection of your central heating directly to the dishwasher. This can also shorten the time for the program. When installing the hot water connection, make sure that the lines are as short as possible to reduce heat losses in the hot water pipes.

But beware! You should do this only if the dishwasher is suitable for it! If you were to do this with an unsuitable dishwasher, you would profit in the short term, but risking losing your device. From a total of four rinses, only two hot water is used: in the main rinse and in the rinse cycle. In the intermediate rinses, which normally use cold water, the grease may dissolve easily with hot water and may clog the dishwasher completely over time.

Set the dishwasher to the correct water hardness, this increases the efficiency and the dishwasher has a longer life. In addition, there is a possibility that you can use it more sparingly and you consume less salt.

Pay attention to which program you use. With the economy button, the shortcut key or an eco program, you can save a lot on lightly soiled dishes. For the one who uses 50°C instead of 60°C during a rinse process save about 25% on energy costs[8]

If you have a program that will dry your dishes, avoid using them. Let it dry naturally over night, use towels or just leave the door of the device after the rinse open. The drying program requires additional energy to heat the dishwasher and you pay for that energy.

The residual sieve should be cleaned regularly. If the strainer is free, the water can drain easily and the water pump runs less.

Before the wastewater runs off, some dishwashers use the hot rinse water with so-called latent storage tanks or with heat accumulators to reuse the heat in another rinsing process. This can save up to 20% of electrical energy[9].

The most efficient way to run a dishwasher is when it is fully loaded. This will clean more dishes with the same amount of water and electricity. If you want to go fast, you can alternatively choose the program with half load.

Nevertheless, you should not exceed the capacity of the machine. As a result, the cleanliness of your dishes suffers because the water cannot reach all the

---

8   [11] (kueche-co.de)

9   [27]

dishes an in addition the lifespan of your appliance suffers.

If possible, avoid pre-washing the dishes by hand in the sink, as well as the pre-wash program. The dishwasher can easily remove most of the dried food leftovers. The water you can save literally.

Dishwasher	
Saving opportunities	**Support for your decision-making**
Hot water connection	In particular, you benefit from central heating if you connect the dishwasher directly to the hot water connection. (Should only be done for suitable dishwashers!)
Location	For hot water connections, use the shortest possible lines.
Water hardness	Set the dishwasher to the correct water hardness.
Economy button / short button Program	Use the economy button, short button, or eco-program, especially on lightly soiled dishes. For the one who uses 50°C instead of 60°C saves about 25% on energy costs.
Drying program	If you have a program that

	will dry your dishes, avoid it. Let it dry naturally.
Strainer	Clean the strainer regularly, so that the water can drain easily and the pump runs less.
Loading	If possible, always wash fully loaded or alternatively, if you want to go fast, choose the program with half load (if available). Nevertheless, the capacity of the machine should not be exceeded.
Prewash	Pre-rinsing the dishes by hand with water is usually not necessary. This water can be saved. It's the same with the pre-wash program. If possible, avoid it.
Machine vs. rinsing by hand	According to a study, there is water saving with a dishwasher in contrast to the hand wash of 50%

	and power savings of 28%.
Potential savings per year	Approximately 20 € per year.
New device	Exchange of old device is recommended after 15 years at the latest.

Table 5: Savings options and support for decision-making for the dishwasher.

Work principle dishwasher

Below you can find a schematic picture of how the dishwasher works (Figure 5). Thus, you can better understand the explanations shown here. To rinse the dishes you need a fresh water pipe and after cleaning a sewer pipe. The amount of fresh water is measured by sensors and floats and flows through a softener unit where the water is softened with the help of salt previously added by hand. Here lime and other minerals are removed from the water. According to the program, the water is heated and passed through a pump through hoses in the rotating arms. By the way, these arms are driven by the water pressure itself and there is no need to spend extra energy on it. It should be noted here that the rotating arms always have to move freely. Otherwise, a breakage or defect of the machine is risked. The dirty water is collected in the sump and filtered through filters on the bottom and used again in the next rinse. The leftovers are collected in a container and later fed to the sewage of the sewage system.

Before the wastewater runs off, some dishwashers use the hot rinse water with so-called latent storage tanks or with heat accumulators to reuse the heat in another rinsing process. This can save up to 20% of electrical energy[10].

The dishwasher lid opens and the detergent dissolves in the warm rinse water. This is used to clean the dishes.

At the end the dishes will be rinsed with fresh water. This rinse aid is supplied and the dishes come clean without drips from the machine.

The drying process differs depending on the machine, but most of the time the residual heat of the rinse water is used to dry the dishes. Or the rinse water is heated to even higher temperatures.

10 [27]

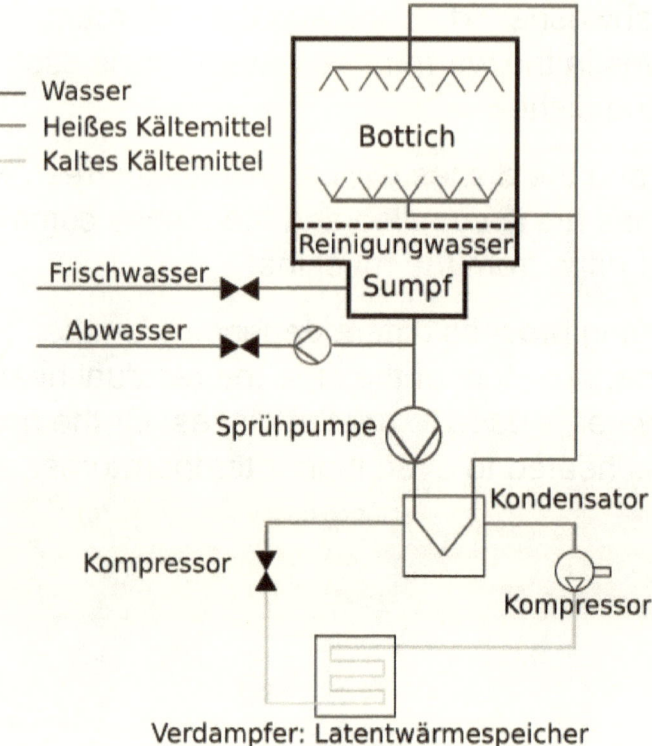

Figure 5: Working principle of the dishwasher.

Energy label dishwasher

Figure 6 shows the energy labeling for dishwashers. It includes the trademark or the name of the manufacturer with the model name (1), the energy efficiency class (2) and the energy consumption in kilowatt-hours (kWh) per year (3). 280 rinses per year are calculated. The actual consumption depends on your usage. In addition you can see at a glance the water consumption in liters per year (4) (same assumption with 280 rinses), the classification of the effect of drying (5), the number of place settings with a standard load (6) and the volume in decibels (dB) (7).

For the dishwasher the best energy efficiency is currently class A+++. The classes A to D are currently no longer available. From 2020, all energy labels will be standardized again to classes A to G.

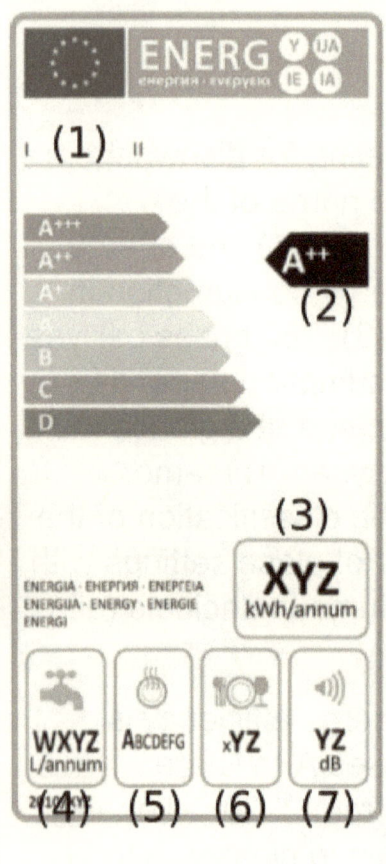

1) Trademark or name of the manufacturer with model name.

2) Energy efficiency class.

3) Energy consumption in kilowatt hours (kWh) per year. Assumption: 280 rinses per year, actual consumption depends on your use.

4) Water consumption in liters per year. Assumption: 280 rinses per year, actual consumption depends on your use.

5) Classification of the effect of drying.

6) Number of place settings for standard load.

7) Volume in decibels

	(dB). Note on dishwashers: The best energy efficiency class is A+++. The classes A to D are currently no longer available. From 2020 on, all energy labels will be standardized again to classes A to G.

Figure 6: Energy label for dishwasher.

The oven

The oven looks back on a more than 6,000 years old history. The first ovens were used in Egypt, where you should rather speak of baking rooms or bake houses. They were located separately outside the buildings and were fired with palm waste and straw. There was an opening in the top of the house. The flatbreads were placed outside on the building and were baked like this.

The Romans continued to develop the oven and built it out of stone. This gave it a relatively good insulation and kept the heat relatively long. From the Roman Empire, the idea spread throughout Europe and provided people with bread.

The first modern ovens have been around since 1851 and were still fired with wood. After that it slowly switched to oil. As the cities grew and the gas network became widespread, gas ovens were also developed. It was not until the 1930s that electric ovens were developed and sold.

Possibilities and support for your decision making – The oven

The oven is nowadays usually combined with a stove in many households. Either it just stands there and is hardly or not at all used or it is only used for pizzas for baking or for warming up meals. Or it is loved and constantly used for everything.

In addition to the less used wood ovens, gas ovens or electric ovens are most commonly used. If there is a gas connection at home, you should decide for one. This keeps operating costs low because gas is much cheaper than electricity. New gas ovens are equipped with a safety mechanism against unwanted gas leakages. If you forget to turn off the gas and gas flows out - which scares many people - then the oven detects this and automatically turns the gas supply off. In a gas oven, however, the top heat is missing, but can be compensated with circulating air. During low-temperature cooking, minimum temperatures between 100-150°C can be achieved. In general, low-temperature cooking works better with electric ovens. The cooking experts among you should be sure in advance, in which temperature range you want to cook.

For electric ovens, a normal power connection is sufficient. Here, however, you should have the connection carried out by an electrical engineer. Incorrect connections can cause accidents, especially if you need a power connection in combination with a cooktop. Because the oven needs about 3000 watts and a stoven about 7000 watts. A power connection is colloquially used for a three-phase AC voltage. These three interconnected AC voltages allow the transport of electricity in the power lines.

Be careful here and do not save in the wrong places!

For electric ovens pay attention to the presence of the "circulating air" function. This can save you up to 30% in energy[11]. And only if you turn a single switch. Amazing how easy you can save energy, isn't it?

For the product types you can choose between stove, built-in cooker or built-in oven. If you bake a little or just use it for pizzas, consider adding a mini-oven. The savings potential is huge here and at the same time it also requires less space. Not to mention the lower initial cost. A mini oven has some advantages. In addition to buying this to a normal oven can also be profitable so as not to heat up the volume of the large oven for two small breads.

There are three sizes for the net- capacity. The compact size gives you approx. 27 liters, the standard size approx. 55 liters and the large volume up to approx. 75 liters net volume. Decide what you

11   [12] (www.bader.at)

need. Again, as big as necessary and as small as possible.

From which side the door can be opened can be decided. However, such as the refrigerator, it cannot be changed later. You have to decide it before you buy one.

When cleaning, cleaning by hand is still the cheapest way to do. In addition to the hand cleaning, there are three other common types of self-cleaning.

At about 100°C the hydrolytic cleaning, which is also known under "AquaClean" or "EasyClean", starts. Here, water vapor combats the dirt and reduces the smell.

At about twice the temperature, at about 200°C, the catalytic purification can start, also known as "EcoClean" or "self-cleaning catalytic enamel". Here a chemical transformation process of the dirt takes place. The advantage of this method is that it can also be retrofitted.

The best cleaning effect is achieved with the highest temperature, at a whopping 500°C. You have to pay the energy to heat the stove so high with your electricity bill. It is a pyrolytic method, also called "activeClean" or "Pyroluxe®Plus". Here the dirt is literally decomposed.

Try to use these self-cleaning programs as little as possible or not at all. Your electric bill will thank you.

For the energy efficiency class, you should make sure that you have at least one device with an A+. An oven with efficiency class A+++ is about 50% more efficient than a device with energy efficiency class A. With 100 baking operations per year, a ten-year-old appliance consumes approx. 160 kWh (48.80 €), a device with energy efficiency class A approx kWh (€ 30.50) and an oven of efficiency class A +++ approx. 50 kWh (€ 15.25).

Attention: The larger the oven, the higher the energy consumption with the same energy efficiency class. That means a large A+++ oven can have the same consumption as a smaller A+ oven.

Oven	
Possibilities for your decision-making	**Support for your decision-making**
Power connection	**Gas/** wood / electricity
Circulating air	Using circulating air saves you up to 30% of energy in an electric oven.
Connection	A normal power connection is sufficient. With a stove, however, a power connection is necessary. Gas connection for gas stoves necessary.
Product type / type of installation	Self standing stoven built-in stoven built-in oven Mini oven
Net capacity	Compact size: Approx. 27 liters

	Standard dimension: approx. 55 liters Large volume: up to 75 liters
Equipment / Extras	In addition to barbecue, microwave or steam cooking function, many things are possible, therefore for everybody individual.
Door stop	Every side possible. Attention: The side cannot be changed afterwards.
Self-cleaning (goes hand in hand with high energy expenditure)	Pyrolytic up to 500°C ("activeClean" or "Pyroluxe®Plus") (The stove is cleaned by very high energy expenditure, but has the purifying effect.) Catalytically up to 200°C ("EcoClean" / "self-cleaning catalytic enamel") (Dirt chemical conversion process.)

	Can also be retrofitted).
	Hydrolytic up to 100°C ("AquaClean" or "EasyClean")
	(Water vapor combats dirt and reduces odor). Water connection necessary.
Energy efficiency	From energy class A to A+++ (you should have at least an **A+).** The efficiency class A+++ is about 50% more efficient than one with an A.
Annual electricity consumption (100 baking operations)	A+++: 50 kWh A++: 70 kWh A+: 80 kWh A: 100 kWh Old appliance: 160 kWh (10 Jahre) Attention: The larger the oven, the higher the energy consumption with the same energy

	efficiency class.
Acquisition cost	From about 150 € to over 7000 € possible.
Savings potential with new purchase	30 € saving potential per year.

Table 6: Possibilities and support for your decision-making for the oven.

Saving tips Oven

If you have an oven with circulating air function, you should use this function as often as possible. Alone with this you save up to 30%, since the oven has to heat with this function 20°C to 30°C (!) less[12].

If you want to save electricity you can use your oven without preheating. The manufacturers use this to achieve a standardization of baking recipes, as everybody has a different oven. If you taste the difference in the dish, you are one of the few people. You can save up to 15% on energy. Not to mention the energy you waste, if you have not prepared everything yet and the oven just keeps heating up unnecessarily. With a typical output of 3000 watts for an oven and an average electricity price of 30.5 cents per kWh, you pay about 1.5 cents per minute. For 15 minutes this makes 23 cents, for one hour 91 cents. If you bake 100 times a year and preheat 15 minutes each time, you pay a whopping 23 € more per year for pre-heating.

However, if a dish should be crispy, it is advisable to preheat it for the taste, otherwise the taste of the dish may change due to the slow heating.

---

12   [12] (www.bader.at)

You can safely switch off the oven 15 minutes before the end of the baking time. It keeps its heat during this time while you are using it. This makes about the same calculation as above with 100 baking operations in the year about € 23 a year.

Make sure that the glazing of the oven is suitable for the existing heat and is tight. Most of the heat is lost there. A triple glazing should be preferred instead of a double glazing.

Open the door as little as possible during baking. If you only open the oven door three times in one hour, the energy requirement increases by up to 10%[13].

Use the self-cleaning programs as little as possible. Especially the pyrolytic cleaning uses with its 500°C very much energy. Avoid this very high energy consumption. If you wash the oven by hand, each time you save up to 5 kWh (about 1.50 €).

Empty the oven from any metal sheets that you do not need. The oven must unnecessarily heat them up additionally. Additional baking trays can require up to 20% more energy.[14]

Dark, black lacquered and enamelled[15] bakeware can absorb heat better than bright bakeware.

---

13   [13] (Backofen und Ceranfeld)

14 [26] (Umweltbundesamt)

Because the black color interacts with more wavelengths. As a result, the sheets heat up faster and you save energy.

The baking molds should also lie flat on the sheet and have straight sides. As a result, the heat gets better to the dish.

Thaw frozen food at room temperature for a long time and do not use the oven or the microwave. When you bake thawed foods, you also consume much less energy than when you start baking them frozen.

Be inventive and tactical. Cook several dishes at once and use the different heights in the oven. With circulating air, the same temperature prevails everywhere. In the case of top and bottom heat, however, the same temperature prevails only in the middle, since the sheet of both heaters (top and bottom) has the same distance.

Clean your oven regularly to remove fatty deposits. You can put a bowl of water on the bottom plate and heat the oven up to 150 degrees. The steam spreads and dissolves the burned-in remains. Then just let the device cool down and wipe with a damp cloth. If you squeeze out lemons and put the bowls in the water, the cleaning will work even better and your oven will have a more pleasant smell.

---

15 Enamel is a ceramic compound similar to glass. It consists of quartz, feldspar, clay, magnesia and borax.

Cleaning your oven regularly extends the life of your device and protects you from a technical failure. In addition, the dirt behaves like an insulation and the oven needs to heat more to bring the oven to the same temperature.

If you own a mini oven, use it instead of the large oven. To warm up buns or to make them crunchy you should prefer a toaster. This can save you up to 70% energy. Because heating the entire volume of the oven requires a lot of energy.

For the energy efficiency class, you should make sure that you have at least an energy class with A+. An oven with efficiency class A+++ is approximately 50% more efficient than a device with A. For 100 baking operations per year, a 10-year-old appliance consumes approx. 160 kWh, a device with energy efficiency class A approx. 80 kWh and an oven of efficiency class A+++ approx. 40 kWh.

Oven	
Saving tips	**Help for your decision making**
Circulating air	If possible, use circulating, as the oven must heat 20°C to 30°C less. This saves up to

	30% on energy.
Preheating	**Do not preheat.** You can keep the dish approximately five minutes more in the oven. This saves up to **20%** energy. (For *crispy* dishes preheating is sometimes necessary).
Shutdown time	Turn off the oven up to **15 minutes earlier**. The oven has nearly the same temperature for this period.
Glazing	A **triple glazing** should be preferred instead of a double glazing.
Opening of the door	Open the door as little as possible during baking. Opening three times per hour increases the energy requirement by about 10%.
Pyrolytic purification	Use the pyrolytic and automatic cleaning programs as less as possible or at best not at all. Very high energy consumption!

	Washing by hand saves up to five kWh each time.
Content	Empty the oven from any metal sheets that you do not need. To heat the unused sheets up to 20% more energy can be needed.
Black bakeware	Dark, black lacquered and enamelled bakeware and plates can absorb the heat better and keep it better. Use flat bakeware with straight sides.
Thawing	Thaw frozen food at room temperature, do not use the oven for it. When you bake thawed foods you also need much less energy.
Tactical approach	Be inventive and tactical. Cook several dishes at once and use the different heights in the oven.
Fatty deposits	Regularly clean the oven. Fat deposits act like an

	insulation.
Alternatives	Mini oven Or use **toaster** for the rolls (**70% savings potential**).
Energy efficiency	From energy class B to A+++ (it should have at least an A+). An efficiency class A+++ device is about 50% more efficient than a device with A.
Potential savings per year	Approximately 45 € per year.
New device	Exchange of old equipment is recommended after 15 years at the latest.

Table 7: Savings tips and support for your decision-making for the oven.

Function principle oven

The functioning of a baking oven is simple. Electricity is sent through a tubular heater (1) (resistance heating). By friction of the current (electrons) with the tubular heater (resistance) heat is generated. If there is a lot of heat it gets hot and this heat is used for heating.

In the "top heat" function, only the upper tubular heater is heated, with "bottom heat" (below the oven bottom) only the lower tubular heater is heated in the bottom (2) and with the "top and bottom heat" both tubular heaters are heated.

With the "circulating air" function, the air is sucked in by a fan (3) located in the rear wall of the oven and laterally blowing out through slots (indicated by red arrows). This creates an artificial convection (circulating air).

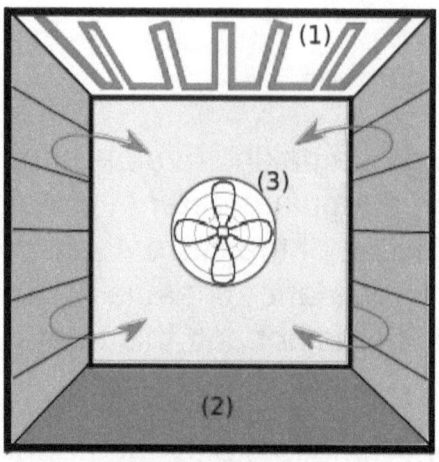

Figure 7: Working principle of an oven.

The function "Grilling" usually uses the same radiator as the top heat.

In the case of an oven with integrated microwave, there is a microwave device for generating and distributing electromagnetic waves.
In combination mode, the cooking time is reduced by approx. 40%.

In an integrated "steam cooking system" the oven needs a water supply, which solve the manufacturers differently. Sometimes a water connection is needed, sometimes a tank needs to be filled manually or it will be solved differently.

Energy label – Oven

Figure 8 shows the energy label for an oven. Here you can see the trademark or the name of the manufacturer with the model name (1), the energy source (2), the energy efficiency class (3), the cooking volume in liters (4) and the energy consumption in kilowatt hours (kWh) per year (5). Here are two assumptions made. On the one hand a standard baking with the heating conventional, on the other hand, a standard baking with the air convection function. For gas ovens, the energy consumption in mega joules (MJ) is additionally indicated.

For the oven the best energy class is currently A+++. The worst energy efficiency class is B. From 2020, the minimum requirement for home baking ovens is energy efficiency class A.

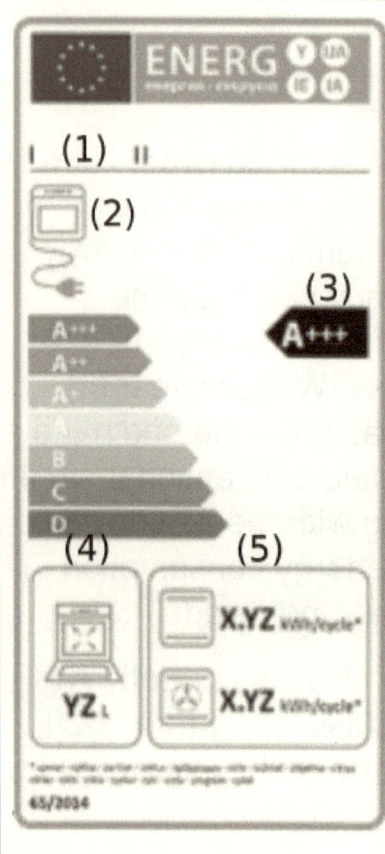

1) Trademark or name of the manufacturer with model name.

2) Power Source, Electricity (Shown) or Gas.

3) Energy efficiency class.

4) Cooking chamber volume in liters.

5) Energy consumption in kWh per standard baking process for the heating modes conventional (upper picture) and with circulating air (lower picture).
For gas ovens, the energy consumption in megajoules (MJ) is additionally

| | indicated.

Note to the oven:

For the oven the best energy class is currently A+++. The worst energy efficiency class is B. From 2020, the minimum requirement for baking ovens is energy efficiency class A. |
| --- | --- |
| *Figure 8: Energy label for the oven.* | |

The stove

A stove or kitchen stove is a device for cooking or frying food. It can be said that the first "stove" originated around 1,000,000 (1 million) years ago when people learned to use and store the fire. Whether one can speak of a stove here is certainly questionable. Nevertheless, the principle is the same.

For the time being, they put stone slabs under the fire, but not in the house itself, but it took place outside in the open air. Then they put the fire higher to make it more back friendly.

The first clay hearths were found in present-day Greece, which the people used there about 30,000 years ago.

When apartments were built and the people settled down, the fireplace moved into the apartment, which, however, brought certain disadvantages with it, such as soot, stench and smoke inside the apartment.

In the 16th century, the first closed stoves came and from the 18th century, the first lowerings were included in the stove to put the pots there. It was not until the 19th century that such stoves circulated as we know them. They were made with a flap to close and were connected with a pipe to the chimney.

Since then, the stoves have been constantly developing.

Possibilities & support for your decision-making

There is no energy label for a stove alone. It is only available for an oven-stove combination. The energy consumption values within a technology such as the induction, the mass hotplates or the radiant heaters are so close that a differentiating classification is unjustifiable.

As a guideline, you can assume the following power values for a four-plate cooker, which of course may vary slightly depending on the model:

A high speed cooker with approx. 2.5 kW, a saving hob with approx. 1 kW and two additional hobs with approx. 1.7 kW.

If you save money here, you should do it like the professional chefs and resorts and choose a gas stove. The fast availability of heat, the good dosage of the gas flame and its low operation costs are some of its many advantages. The most common form in Germany, however, is the electric stove. Alternatives can be found in solid fuel stoves, such as wood. However, these special forms are not discussed in detail here.

A normal power connection is sufficient for a 90 cm size. For larger models, however, a power connection is necessary.

For example, you can buy a two-piece hotplate cheap and put it almost anywhere. Take care that there is enough space above the hob due to the heat. There is a risk of fire here.

The market offers various hob types. The electric hob, the glass ceramic hob and the gas hob, the cheapest option. The classic mass cooking field is still widely used. These hot-cast iron hotplates are equipped with normal hotplates or flash hotplates with increased performance. The most modern variant is the induction hob. Compared to a glass ceramic hob, however, an induction hob does not pay for itself within 15 years due to the higher initial costs. You may also have to buy the cookware, because not every pot is suitable for induction.

If a person cooks on the stove for 45 minutes a day, a new appliance will consume about 150 kWh (45.75 €) and with a ten-year old appliance about 300 kWh (91.50 €) per year. The message in this example is: A new stove consumes half the energy of a ten year old device.

Stove	
Possibilities for a new stove	**Support for your decision-making**
Power connection	Gas Electricity Solid fuel
Connection	A normal power connection is sufficient. From 90cm size, however, a high power connection is necessary. Gas connection with gas stoves
Product type / type of installation	Stove Cooker set Range Cooker (very large) Self-standing Table stove
Hob type	Electric hob Gas hob

	Mass hob Ceramic hob Induction hob The cheapest one is a gas hob.
Energy efficiency	For a stove only, no energy label is available. Only for an oven / stove set. Four-plate cooker power values (slight deviations depending on stove model possible): 1 x 2.5 kW (fast cooking field) 1 x 1 kW (energy saving field) 2 x approx. 1.7 kW
Annual electricity consumption (2 persons, about 2 hours per week)	New appliance: approx. 110 kWh-150 kWh Old device: 200 kWh (10 years old)
Acquisition cost	From about 80 € to over 10,000 € possible.

Saving potential with new purchase	30 € saving potential per year.

Table 8: Possibilities for a new stove and support for your decision-making.

Saving tips stoven

Even with the stove you can save a lot of money. For example, use the smallest possible pot and pan size for food. Put this pot on the appropriate hotplate. Ideally, it corresponds exactly to the size of the pot or pan bottom. Every centimeter that the pot is smaller than the stove plate leads to 20% to 30% more consumption[16].
If possible, use pressure cookers. Only by using this special pot you save up to 50% energy and up to 70% time[17]. A pressure cooker has even more advantages: By cooking, many of the minerals, vitamins and flavor are retained. In addition, the odors remain in the pot and are not distributed in the kitchen. The safety valve is also intended for your safety, as it automatically opens when the pressure is too high.

For normal pots, use the matching lid. This can save you another 30% in energy.

The thinner and more thermally conductive the material of the pot and the pan, the less heat is needed to heat the conductive medium (pot and

---

16   [14] (Bayerisches Staatsministerium für Umwelt und Verbraucherschutz)

17   (Backofen und Ceranfeld)

---

pan). Because this distributes the heat in the cookware much faster.

However, it also keeps the heat less. To compensate this, the dishes should have a double-walled bottom and lid. These saves the heat better.

Kettles are more efficient than electric stoves. For amounts of water up to 400-500 milliliters you should use a kettle. Everything over half a liter makes more sense with pots. If you want to boil water in the pot, save about 50% with gas instead of electricity.

When cooking with a lid, little water is enough. The food does not have to be completely covered with water. The unused water does not need to be heated, which saves you time and money.

Thaw frozen food prematurely at room temperature and do not thaw it with the cooker. That costs you a lot of unnecessary energy.

At the beginning, turn the stove to a high level and let the meal continue to simmer at a lower level. Finally, you can turn off the stove a few minutes earlier to take advantage of the residual heat.

Stove	
Saving possibilities	**Support for your decision making**
Pots & Pans	Use small pots and pans. Choose a suitable cooking plate for the pan. If possible use the smallest cooking plate. Pots and pans should be adapted to the content (not too big). Use pressure cookers (50% energy saving).
Lid & Size	Cooking with lid saves 30%. If the size of the pot is the same as the hob, this will save you 30%.
Pot types	Use thin and thermally conductive dishes with double-walled floors and lids.
Kettle vs. electric	**Kettles** are more efficient

stove	than electric stoves. For up to 400-500 ml use the kettle.
Cooking	When cooking with a lid, little water is enough. The food does not have to be completely covered with water.
Heating up	Premature frozen foods at room temperature.
Residual heat	Use residual heat.
Potential savings per year	Approximately 15 € saving potential per year.
New device	Exchange of old equipment is recommended after 15 years at the latest.

Table 9: Savings options and support for your decision-making for the stove.

Function-principle stove

As with the oven electric current is sent through a conductor (resistance heating in red), which heats up and gets hot. By an annular stringing of the conductor this effect is amplified, which is why cooking plates are round. The ladder is usually rotated like a spiral so that as many ladders as possible can be packed in a small space.

Figure 9: How a stove works.

Energy Label for the stove - Not available

For the stove alone, there is no energy label. This only exists for the oven or for an oven-stove combination. The energy consumption values within a technology such as the induction, the mass hotplates or the radiant heaters are so close that in respect to the energy consumption a differentiating classification is not justifiable.

The microwave

A coincidence and the right thoughts led to the invention of the microwave.

In 1946, the engineer Percy Spencer researched in the laboratory of the American armor group Raytheon. He stopped at a magnetic field tube of a radar to inspect something. As he reached into his jacket pocket, he held his chocolate bar in his hand, which was melted and sticky. He did not notice any heat source. He realized that the reason must lie in the magnetic wave tube. The principle of the microwave was discovered.

It was not until 1954 that the first microwave oven was sold for a whopping $ 2000, if you call it a microwave. It weighed as much as 750 kg in the size of a freezer. It was not until the mid-1960s when the microwave was introduced to private households.

Since the 60s, the microwave has been constantly developing and improving. You can therefore choose between a standard microwave or a combination microwave. In the last mentioned device a grill is contained, in some also a circulating air function or even a steam cooking function. Other options include upper and lower heat, display, timer and defrost function.

The latest development is a microwave with inverter function. An inverter helps that the power output remains constant even at very low power. Normally the power is switched on and off. For example, if a microwave has a maximum power of 800 W, but you have set only 600 W, the magnetron in which the microwaves are generated is always turned off. Basically it is constantly heated with the maximum power and waited in between until it has reached an average of 600 W. With an inverter, it is possible to control exactly the set power you choose. So the energy is used optimally. In addition, a particularly gentle cooking process is created, which makes it possible to heat even sensitive foods.

Microwaves can be purchased with a stainless steel, plastic, or metal housing and a capacity between 13 liters and 45 liters. The most common powers are between 700 W and 2000 W, which in turn can be adjusted from three to more than eleven power levels. If you would use the microwave for half an hour at 1000 W every day, you would have costs of about 55 € per year (should be seen as an example calculation). At three minutes a day, this would cost around € 5.50.

Decision-making possibilities & Support four your decision making – The microwave

Microwave	
Decision-making possibilities	**Support for your decision-making**
Product type	Microwave Combination microwave (grill)
Design type	Standing device Built-in device
Functions	Grill Re-circulation function Two-sided heat function Display Timer Defrost function Steam cooking function
Microwave with inverter technology	An inverter works so that the power output remains constant even at very low

	power (usually the microwave is switched on and off). In this case the energy is used optimally.
Net capacity	From 13 liters to over 45 liters.
	The larger the microwave, the higher the consumption, especially as an oven replacement.
	(In normal use, up to 20 liters are suitable).
Material housing	Stainless steel
	Plastic
	Metal
Adjustable power levels	From 3 to over 11 levels.
Power	From 700 W to over 2000 W.
Annual electricity consumption (45 minutes per week with 1000 watts)	Approximately 12 € per year.

Acquisition cost	From about 40 € to over 3000 € possible.
Savings potential with new purchase	5 € savings potential per year.

Table 10: Decision-making possibilities & Support four your decision making – The microwave.

Saving tips for the Microwave

For small amounts up to 400 grams or milliliters, the microwave is more favorable for heating up something than the electric stove, because the stove must first be heated up the pot. To boil water the kettle, however, is the cheaper option, because the microwave has only an efficiency of about 65%. Heating one liter of water a day would save you about € 5 per year. For 100 ml per day that would be about 50 cents a year.

The best thing is stil thawing food without any device and thawing the still cold goods for their own in the room temperature.

Mostly by pressing a key combination the devive can be secured against unwanted use, such as in front of children. With it you avoid unnecessary power consumption, if the child unintentionally turns on the microwave or opens the door (lamp is on). Old appliances in particular consume energy even when they are in stand-by mode, especially when the light is on when the door is open. Therefore, you should turn off the microwave completely. For this purpose a power strip with integrated on-off switch can be useful.

Cover plates or bowls with a microwave hood. With it the heat can not escape and in most cases a shorter heating time is sufficient.

Warm the food directly on the dishes from which you will eat. When decanting or redeployment thus no heat is lost.

In the meantime, stir again and again, because the microwaves only penetrate about three to six centimeters into the food. This only heats the surface and it takes longer for the food to heat evenly. At the same time, the food can overheat on the outside and can damage the food.

For fast thawing up to 400 grams, you should use the microwave in terms of energy. Everything over 400 grams should be cooked in the pot on the stove.

Microwave	
Saving possibilities	**Support for your decision-making**
Microwave vs. stove	For small amounts (rule of thumb: up to 400 grams / milliliter), the microwave is cheaper than the stove.
Microwave vs. kettle	To boil water the kettle is the cheaper option, because the microwave has an efficiency of about 65%. Savings potential about 5 € per year (with one liter a day).
Childlock	Mostly by pressing a key combination the device can be secured against unwanted use (such as children).
Switch off	Old appliances consume energy even when in stand-by mode, especially when the light is on, when

	the door is open. Completely switch off the microwave.
Lid	Cover plates or bowls with the microwave hood.
Avoid transferring	Warm the food directly on the dishes from which you will eat. When transferring heat is lost.
Stirring	In the meantime, stir again and again. Because microwaves heating up the food only about three to six inches into the food.
Thawing	When fast thawing for about 400 grams use the microwave. But the best to do is to thaw without any appliance and let the cooled goods thaw themselves.
Energy efficiency	Look here for the maximum power. 1000 watts are sufficient for the

	average consumer.
Potential savings per year	Approximately 10 € per year.
New device	Exchange of old device is recommended after 15 years at the latest.

Table 11: Saving possibilities and support for your decision-making for the microwave.

Function principle – The microwave

As the name implies, the microwave oven works with the help of microwaves, without any direct contact with a source of heat, as is the case with the ordinary cooker, the grill, and so on.

These waves have a wavelength of about twelve cm. This corresponds to about two billion oscillations per second. This wavelength excites polar molecules, especially water, this means, they are set in motion. There is also a resistance or friction between the molecules and while the molecules are moving, the friction generates heat. This heat heats the food. The waves penetrate about three to six centimeter into the food. Until then, they have already interacted with food.

Generation of microwaves:

In a so-called magnetron (6) electrons are guided by means of magnets on circular paths. As a result, they send out microwaves, among other things. The number of emitted microwaves can be increased by means of cavities at the edge of the circular path. The efficiency of a magnetron is about 70%. That means 70% of the electrical energy is converted into microwaves.

A portion of the microwaves generated is guided to the outside by means of an antenna and coupled via a waveguide (5) into the microwave (4). Within the device, the microwaves are spread over a reflector wing (3) so that they reach the food from all sides. The reflector wing is located behind the cover plate (2). The food is usually on a turntable, which is attached to the bottom plate (1). In addition, in a microwave there are also a transformer (8) and a cooling fan (7).

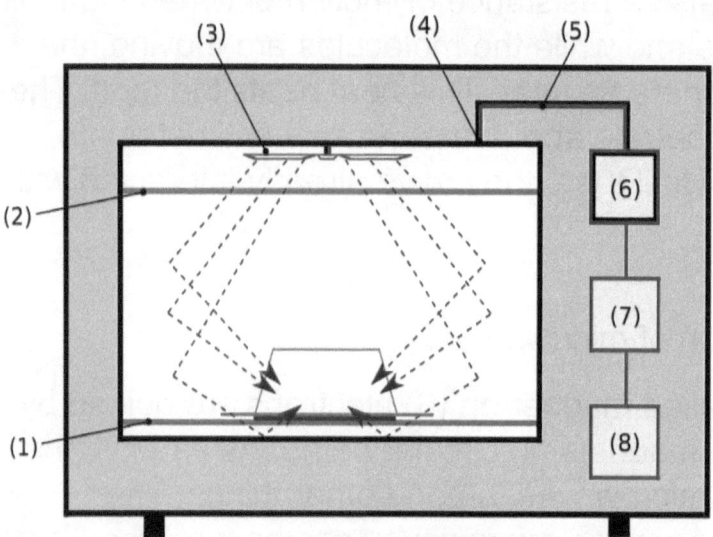

Figure 10: How a microwave works.

1) base plate, 2) cover plate, 3) reflector wings, 4) microwaves, 5) waveguide, 6) magnetron, 7) cooling fan, 8) transformer.

Energy label Microwave - Not available

There is no energy label for the microwave.

The kettle

Before the first electric kettle was presented at the World's Fair in Chicago, there were already water boilers that heated water. When the very first kettle was invented is not certain, just as not who invented it. Nevertheless, the kettle was developed to just one heating element.

You can choose between glass, plastic, metal and stainless steel. The plastic case, especially on newly purchased devices, can cause an unpleasant plastic smell. In addition, there is a risk that harmful components such as PAH-polycyclic aromatic hydrocarbons, bisphenol A (BPA) or plasticizers (phthalates) can enter the water. A test by Stiftung Warentest in 2012 showed that after 24 hours of continuous use no danger to humans existed. Nevertheless, sporadic amounts of BPA were detected, but below the maximum value of the European Food Safety Authority (EFSA).

Therefore, for yours safety's sake, refrain from the cheapest products. High quality appliances are still not expensive, but offer health and technical (automatic safety shutdown) security. Here you should not save money on the wrong things.

In addition to capacities of 0.6 to 3 liters, you can choose between powers of 100 watts to 2400 watts. In general, the higher the power, the faster the water boils. An average water heater with about 1.5 liters capacity has about 2000 watts and brings a liter of water to boil in about three minutes.

Look at energy efficiency for maximum performance. As a rule of thumb, you can accept the following. It should be about 1000 watts to a liter of capacity. From two liters capacity, it should be about 2000 watts.

In terms of energy, make sure that the kettle is double-walled, has an automatic switch-off and the temperature can be regulated. Concealed heating elements also give you the certainty that no particles get into the water from the heating coil. In addition, you can choose from various equipments: Replaceable lime filter, lighting, level indicator, keeping warm function or signal at cooking point.

You should also make sure that there is a strainer or filter at the pouring spout to catch the lime.

There is a minimum capacity for kettles. Pay attention to the smallest possible filling quantity. Most kettles have about 0.5 liters. If possible take one with 0.25 liters. The smaller the better, so that only the water that you need is heated.

Decision-making possibilities & Support for your decision-making for the Kettle

Kettle	
Decision-making possibilities	**Support for your decision-making**
Material	Glass Plastic Stainless steel Metal
Net capacity	From 0.6 liters to 3 liters.
Power	From 100 watts to 2400 watts.
Equipments & options	Double wall Temperature adjustable Replaceable lime filter **Automatic shutdown** (pay attention to short shutdown time) Lighting Concealed heating elements

	Scale filter
	Level indicator
	Keeping warm function (high energy consumption)
	Signal at cooking point
Sieve / filter	There should be a strainer or filter against the lime at the pouring spout.
Minimum capacity	If possible, pay attention to the smallest possible filling quantity. The most kettles have 0.5 liters. 0.25 liters are better.
Energy efficiency	Look here for maximum performance. Rule of thumb: Up to one liter of capacity should have about 1000 watts. From two liters on, it should have about 2000 watts.
Annual electricity	Approximately 5 € per

consumption (10 minutes per week with 2000 watts)	year.
Acquisition cost	From about 10 € to over 300 € possible.
Saving potential with new purchase	Approximately 50% saving potential per year of annual consumption when used for heating water instead of microwave or stove.

Table 12: Decision-making possibilities and support for your decision-making for the kettle.

Saving tips for the kettle

If you do not know whether you should use the kettle or the stove, you can remember this rule of thumb. For quantities up to 400 milliliters, the kettle is cheaper than the electric stove.

Decalcify the kettle regularly. This increases the product life. Calcification reduces performance, increases power consumption and can damage the heating elements. It is recommended to descale the kettle every three months.
There are chemical products for decalcification in the market. It is easier and less expensive with vinegar (essence) or citric acid, which you can buy in almost every market. Dilute the ingredients with water and fill it in the device and let it act for half an hour. Then rinse well with clean water so that no residues remain.

As soon as the water boils, the kettle should switch itself off automatically. This saves energy and is important for your safety.

If available, use the temperature controller. Mostly 100°C are not needed. The green tea, for example, only needs about 60°C. This saves time and energy. You should use such win-win situations.

Boil only as much water as you need. Otherwise, the extra water is unnecessarily heated. For example, to measure the water fill it first into the cup and then into the kettle.

Kettle	
Saving possibilities	**Support for your decision-making**
Kettle vs. stove	For quantities up to 400 milliliters, the kettle is cheaper than the stove.
Decalcification	Decalcificate the kettle regularly. This increases the product life.
Automatic shutdown	Once the water boils, the kettle should automatically turn itself off. This saves energy and is safer!
Thermostat	Often 100°C is not needed. For example, green tea only needs about 60°C. Use a thermostat!
Amount of water	Only heat the water what you need. For example, fill the water in the cup

	and then into the kettle.
Savings potential per year	Approximately 5 € saving potential per year.
New device	There is no recommended number of years for the exchange of your old kettle.

Table 13: Saving possibilities and support for your decision-making for the kettle.

Function principle for the kettle

As with the oven or the stove, electricity is sent to the kettle through a conductor or heating element (resistance heating). This heats up and gets hot. The heating element is often positioned directly in the water, which increases the efficiency. As a result, it is also prone to calcifications. The heating element can also dissolve substances and pass into the water. Therefore, you can choose a kettle, where the heating element is located in the bottom (with lower efficiency then of course).

Noise of a kettle - origin

Shortly after switching the kettle on, it already makes sounds that reminds you of a hissing sound. When the bubbles on the water surface are visible, the noise disappears and the bubbling and boiling begin. But why is it like that?

Even if the water is still cold shortly after switching the kettle on, tiny water vapor bubbles are already be formed on the bottom. This is because the heating elements are on the bottom and the water is heated there first. The heat, however, can not spread as quickly as it is heated. In some areas, the water can now change from liquid to gaseous state within fractions of a second. These mini explosions cause a part of the noise.

This rapid formation of the bubbles has their cause in the boiling delay. The actual boiling point of water is 100°C. However, if the water is heated very quickly, it can become over 100°C without evaporating. A little vibration is enough and the overheated water evaporates abruptly and explodes, causing a noise again.

If the bubbles become larger as a result of more heat, they also rise further upwards, where they then reach cold water. As a result, a part of the water vapor of the bubble condenses, thereby reducing the pressure inside. This happens so fast that the bubble implodes. This is exactly what causes the bulk of the noise.

The kettle is thus getting hotter and the bubbles can grow and continue to rise up until they finally reach the water surface and burst there. That's what you see the bubbling and boiling.

Energy Label for the electric kettle - Not available

There is no energy label for the kettle.

The toaster

Before electric toasters were toasted, bread slices were roasted over the open fire. The Egyptians as well as the Romans did this to make the bread more aromatic and durable. Through the Romans, this tradition spread throughout most of Europe.

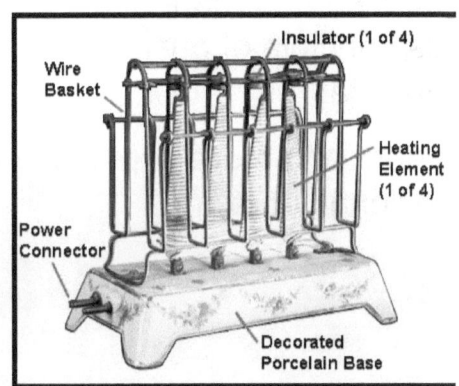

Figure 11: The first patent-pending toaster[18].

As electricity became more normal, so did the electric toasters. Around 1906, the American George Schneider filed the first patent for a toaster named "Heating conductor of suitable resistance wire". As it often happens with new inventions, the sales volume was not quite high.

It was not until 1908 when the American company General Electric launched the model D-12 that it was successfully sold to households. The device still

18   [15] (History, 2014)

worked with a wire rack, which had to be turned over by hand. Therefore, many also burned their fingers on it. The first so-called "pop-up toaster" was produced and marketed in 1926 by Toastmaster. This principle of pushing out the toast has been kept to this day.

Modern and more expensive models have various additional functions.

Decision-making possibilities & Support for your decision-making – The Toaster

You can choose between glass, plastic, stainless steel and a metal housing. There are different sizes and types of toasters. The standard toaster has two slots, but they are also available with one or up to six slots. If you really eat a lot of toast, then you can also choose for a running toaster. But this is not recommended due to the high purchase and electricity costs.

The slots can be purchased with a standard size, but also with extra long, extra deep or extra wide slots. For some toasters the slot width is adjustable.

As an option you can take the bread roll grill as an option. I would recommend this to you, because rolls with the toaster can be much more energy-efficient baked or roasted compared to an oven. There are two options, a plug-in or already integrated grill.

Optionally, there are crumb drawers, which are quite handy for cleaning.

For your own safety, the toaster should have an overheating protection and automatic switch-off at all costs. A warning light helps you to have a quick overview of whether the device is on or off.

Other features include adjustable tanning levels, roast level electronics, keep warm function, defrost function and quick stop function if you have set the toaster too long.

Whether a cable rewind is important to you is up to you.

Toaster	
Decision-making possibilities	**Support for your decision-making**
Material	Glass Plastic Stainless steel Metal
Net capacity	From 1 slot to 6 slots. Running toaster (expensive).
Power	From 300 Watt to 3.000 Watt.
Construction	Extra long slots. Extra deep slots. Extra wide slots. Variable slot width.
Options	Rolls rust attachable integrated

	Crumb drawer
	Automatic shutdown
	Indicator light
	Overheating protection
	Adjustable tanning levels
	Roast-grade electronics
	Warm function
	Defrost
	Quick Stop function
	Cable rewind
Annual electricity consumption (10 minutes per week with 850 watts)	Appr. 2 €.
Acquisition cost	From about 9 € to over 1,000 € possible.
Savings potential with new purchase, when using instead of oven.	At least 5 € saving potential per year.

Table 14: Decision-making possibilities and support for your decision-making for the toaster.

Saving tips Toaster

The toaster plays its strength as an alternative to the oven. The bread rolls are not only baked more energy-efficient, but also finished faster, since not the entire oven interior hast to be heated. At the toaster the rolls directly lies over the heating wires. This can save up to five euros per year.

If you put a foil over the buns, the heat from below is reflected on the foil, which makes the rolls crispier and faster ready.

There are also toasters that have a one-slot toast function. If you want to make just one toast crispy, you can use this feature, saving 50% in energy as only one side is heated.

In addition, toasters should have a function that recognizes whether a toast is present or not. Unfortunately, I could not find such a toaster.

In addition, I could not find a device in which the upper openings close automatically, so as to save energy.

Likewise, in my opinion, the sides of the toaster are getting too hot, which means the insulation is bad. These could be isolated even better.

Energy Label Toaster - Not available

There is no energy label for the toaster.

The extractor hood

In 1940, Vent-A-hood launched the first household extractor hood. Vapors are cooking and baking fumes, which consist essentially of air, water and fat. An extractor hood sucks off these vapors. This includes a housing, a grease filter, with recirculation mode optionally an activated carbon filter, a fan, lighting and a control unit.

Instead of opening the windows in winter and throwing the expensive heated air out of the "window", an extractor hood may also be suitable for saving energy in this context. However, this cannot be said in general terms and depends very much on how often you cook and how often you have to open the windows for it.

On the one hand, there is the exhaust air operation, in which the vapors are passed through the grease filter and are led to the outside via a exhaust pipe. The pipes should be at least 150 millimeters in diameter to allow an adequate air volume flow. Flat channel systems require a minimum output of 500 to 600 m³/h (cubic meters per hour). Fan motors work quieter, but require a higher performance. The exhaust air output is basically the most important thing. The shape and type are also important, but less significant.

The connection to the outside can be carried out with a wall box. Currently, manufacturers still allow a reduction of the diameter with a reducer. In the future, however, more and more manufacturers could ban this. If you did this anyway, you could lose the manufacturer's warranty. In addition, the reduction stresses the engine and its lifespan suffers. This means that you have to renew the engine after a short time, which can cost you additionally. Therefore, it is the best to consider the diameter of the pipe.

It should also be mentioned that the larger the opening, the more the sound noises are reduced.

In order to reduce the operating noise, blowers that are mounted outside the extractor hood are also suitable. Often these are placed on the outside wall. As a result, the air does not have to be pressed through the tubes, but is sucked in, wherein the air resistance is lower and energy can be saved.

Important!

The exhaust air operation is not always possible without danger. If you use a no longer used or decommissioned chimney for exhaust air, this has to be checked by the chimney sweeper. If there is a fireplace in the apartment or if there are open fire places (depending on the room air), a separate gas heating or a gas water heater, health problems can occur! The German fireplaces regulation allows exhaust air operation only if sufficient fresh air is supplied. Because the extractor hood can suck the air in the apartment so strong that a negative pressure can occur. This deprives the fire oxygen, which can produce toxic gases, since the combustion cannot complete due to the lack of oxygen. Under certain circumstances, a so-called extractor hood radio set can help. When the kitchen window is closed, it automatically turns off the hood.

In any case:

Have this checked by a specialist. Your health has priority!

Or you decide for a circulating air extraction. Here the vapors are passed through the grease filter and the activated charcoal filter (expensive) and then led back into the room. The grease filters are nowadays mostly made of metal and are reusable. Avoid fleece filters that need to be bought and replaced after some time. The recirculation option is recommended if, for some reason, you are not allowed to damage the wall. Due to increasingly stringent energy-saving regulations in the construction industry, recirculation-air extraction is becoming increasingly important, especially for low-energy houses and passive houses.

Cooktop extractors

A modern trend is retractable cooktops and downdraft systems. With retractable fume hoods, a wall is raised behind the hob, so that the steam can be sucked directly from the pot. The downdraft systems are integrated directly into the worktop or next to the hob.

The disadvantages of retractable fume hoods and downdraft systems is the high purchase price (about 1000 € to 2000 €). In addition, the devices must be purchased from the same manufacturer, because otherwise they would not fit. There must be a prescribed depth of worktops during installation. In the lower cabinets, there is therefore less space, since this space is needed for the device itself and maybe for your exhaust air. It may be that with the front plates, that the extractor is not sufficient because it is too far away from the hobs. You can work around this problem if you arrange the hobs in series, but this must be planned in advance.

Retractable extractor hoods save space and offer more freedom of view as the extractor hood does not hang in front of the head. Generally, these are also quieter, as the sound is reduced by the base cabinets. The exhaust air is generated directly on the pot, whereby the ambient air in the kitchen is odor-free. In addition, the proximity to the pot also provides good lighting. Especially with a cooking island, the downdraft system offers a very good design and planning freedom.

Retractable extractor hood / Downdraft system	
Advantages	**Disadvantage**
Space-saving	High purchase price
Quietly	Extractor optimally only at full power. Ongoing costs are high.
Exhaust air and lighting near the pot.	Mandatory depth at the worktops necessary for installation.
Design and planning freedom (cooking island)	Extracting lower front plates. Could not be enough. Hobs should be arranged in series.
Free view	Less storage space in the lower cabinets.
Better air, because extraction is directly at the place of origin.	For integrated hoods, the equipment must be purchased from the same manufacturer.

Table 15: Advantages and disadvantages of retractable extractor hoods and downdraft systems.

You can install the downdraft system to the stove in various places, which has certain advantages and disadvantages.

If you place the downdraft next to the hob, you have the option to place it either on the long side or on both short sides of the hob. If this is not the case, it may be that the exhaust air strength for the opposite hobs is not sufficient because it is too far away. After the usage, the downdraft is covered with a simple or hinged lid. This makes this place usable again for other items.

Automatically extendable downdraft systems are usually mounted on the long side of the hobs. The mid-mounted systems are rare.

The main advantage of the fume hood in the middle of the hob is that the downdraft is equidistant to all cooktops and thus can work most effectively. Also, the system does not have to be driven out. This saves space in the base cabinet. However, you also lose working space on the hob.

Cleaning

If noodle water runs into the mouth of the trigger, you do not have to be afraid. Each manufacturer has a container that collects the water, only the volume is different. If you clean the grease filter, you can also empty the container and clean it if necessary. The manufacturers recommend to clean the grease filter on a monthly basis. Depending on the type, this happens either with water and mild detergent or some are even dishwasher safe. The activated carbon filters do not need to be cleaned, but they must be replaced regularly.

Decision-making possibilities & Support for your decision-making

If you have chosen a new extractor fan, you should first choose one of these options: Exhaust air or convection air. As this must already be taken into account in the planning. Then you can decide whether it should be a classic cooker hood or a cooktop extractor or a downdraft system.

The best is to choose a device that is as quiet as possible. The Federal Environmental Agency recommends a maximum of 67 decibels for recirculation hoods and a maximum of 62 decibels for exhaust hoods. But there are already much quieter hoods. Up to 50 dB is a very good value. For comparison: 55 dB equals a rain or a quiet conversation.

With the product types you are spoiled for choice. The range goes from wall, island, ceiling, intermediate and under-hob hood over fan block, corner hood, bowl ventilation and downdraft system. You can also decide between glass, plastic and stainless steel. There are no limits to the design. There are (almost) no limits to the imagination here.

With the equipment, the decision question goes on. There is a touch control and various functions such as 24-hour function. When lighting, make sure that it is an LED lighting. Here you can save up to 80% of energy compared to halogen lamps. With the circulating hoods you opt better for metal grease filters, rather than for fleece filters, because you have to buy the fleece filter. The metal filters can be washed and are usually dishwasher safe. Many hoods also have an intensive function or boost function. Use them sparingly as they have a very high performance. There are also intensive levels with automatic reset that can turn off themselves. You can already buy smarthome-compatible hoods too.

The power goes from 100 watts to over 500 watts. The maximum exhaust air output ranges from 200 m³/h to over 1000 m³/h. The average is about 600 m³/h. Do not choose the exhaust air power too high and calculate how much you need before. As a rule of thumb, 7 times the volume of the room.
Here's an example of how to calculate a reasonable airflow. Let's say the kitchen is 20 m², the ceiling is 2.20 meters high. Then multiply these two sizes and multiply 7 more:

$$20 \text{ m}^2 \text{ x } 2.20 \text{ m x } 7 = 308 \text{ m}^3(/h).$$
(Living space x room height x 7 = required exhaust air output of an extractor hood)

That's the approximate exhaust flow you should choose. The blower levels can be stepless adjustable or have from one to ten levels available.

The acquisition costs goes from 35 € to over 7000 €. Accordingly, designer pieces can be even more expensive.

Extractor hood	
Decision-making possibilities	**Support for your decision-making**
Exhaust system	Extractor hood with exhaust air operation Extractor hood with recirculation mode Cooktop extractor (downdraft systems) Attention: This must already be taken into account in the planning.
Product type	Wall hood Island hood Ceiling hood Intermediate hood Flat hood Base hood Corner hood

	Downdraft system
Material	Glass (partially hardened)
	Plastic
	Stainless steel
Features	Touch Control
	24 hours function
	LED lighting (80% more economical than halogen lamps)
	Metal grease filter (mostly dishwasher-safe)
	Carbon filter
	Plastic filter
	Fleece filter
	Intensive speed
	Intensive level with automatic reset (stop)
	Edge extraction system
	Silence key
	Fully automatic extractor hood

	Hob-based hood control
	Smart Home enabled
Power	From 100 watts to over 500 watts.
Exhaust air flow maximum in m³/h	From 200 m³/h to over 1000 m³/h possible.
	Average about 600 m³/h
	Rule of thumb: about 7 times the volume of the room.
Blower stage	Stepless adjustment.
	From 1 to over 10 levels possible.
	Boost stages also available.
Volume	Maximum 67 dB recommended for recirculation hoods and 62 dB for extractor hoods.
Annual electricity consumption (126 minutes per week with 120 watts)	About 4 €.
Energy	A+++ (about 25

efficiency class	kWh/year)
Information according to energy label	A++ (about 30 kWh/year) A+ (about 35 kWh/ year) A (about 45 kWh/ year) B (about 70 kWh/ year) C (about 90 kWh/ year) D (about 110 kWh/ year) E is from 20.02.2019 not available anymore
Grease separation Efficiency class	A B C D
Acquisition cost	From about 35 € to over 7,000 € possible.
Savings potential with new purchase	At least 5 € saving potential per year. Depending on energy efficiency class difference.

Table 16: Decision-making possibilities and support for your decision-making for cooker hoods.

The wall box

A wall box is the connecting piece between the extractor hood (1) and the connection to the outside. In it, the exhausted air is directed from the kitchen to the outside. The outer cover of a wall box consists of slats, which can often be closed, or a fixed grid (4). In most cases, a fly screens (3) is integrated to prevent the entering of insects. So that the air does not get from outside to the inside a backflow flap (2) is used. Within the wall box and the pipe, condensate (water) may be generated due to the temperature difference between the hot extracted haze and the outside temperature. To transport this condensate, a slight gradient of about two degrees is taken into account.

In Figure 12 you can see a wall box as it is typically constructed. It consists of a backflow flap (2), a fly screen (3) and an oblique outer grille (4). With all these devices, power losses occur. For the backflow flap, it is about 25%, for fly screens depending on the degree of soiling 5-95% and the sloping outer grid about 25% loss of power. The blue lines with arrows (5) represent the draft within the extractor hood (1) and the wall box.

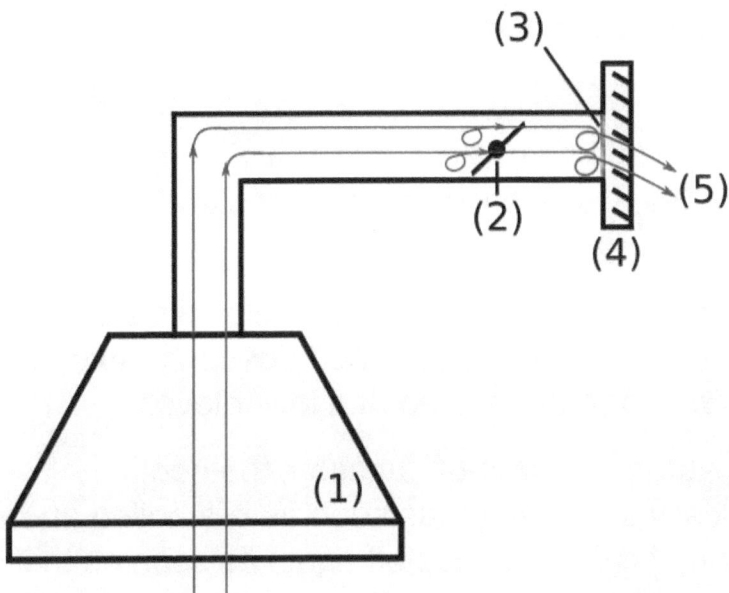

Figure 12: A typical construction of a wall box (with power losses) for an extractor hood (1) with a backflow flap (2) (about 25%), a fly screen (3) (5-95%) and an oblique outer grid (4) (about 25%). The blue lines (5) represents the draft.

Saving tips extractor hood

If possible, use the smallest necessary level. The higher the level, the faster the fan turns and the higher the energy consumption.

Use a lid for pots and pans. As a result, less steam comes out of the pot and the hood does not have to work anyway or can be used at a lower level.

With the automatic shut-off function, the hood automatically switches on as soon as it is boiled and then automatically switches off again as soon as the steam disappears. However, this requires an air sensor that you can upgrade.

If not necessary, leave the light of the hood off or use it as little as possible. In most of them halogen lamps are still installed and they consume much more power than an LED lamp. If possible, replace old halogen lamps with LED lamps. If you use the extractor hood frequently, this can quickly pay for itself.

Clean the grease filters and the fly screen of the wall box regularly. These become more and more obstructed over time and can go so far that they become completely blocked. As a result, the extractor hood tries to force more air through, as the fan rotates faster with more power.

Use wall boxes that only open the shaft when the hood is in operation. Otherwise, cold air gets in from the outside in and the heating costs increase.

If the kitchen is well ventilated, the cooker hood can work more efficiently.

Extractor hood	
Saving possibilities	**Support for you decision-making**
Level	Use the lowest level if sufficient.
Lid	Use a lid for pots and pans.
Automatic shutdown	Once cooked, the cooker hood automatically turns on and off.
Lighting	Use the light of the hood as little as possible.
Cleaning	Clean the grease filters and the fly screen of the wall box regularly.
Wall box	Use wall boxes that only open the shaft when the hood is in operation.
Ventilation	In a well-ventilated kitchen, the device works more efficiently.
Saving potential	Approximately 5 € (With a closed rather than

	open wall box also considerably more, due to the heating costs).

Table 17: Savings possibilities and support for your decision-making for cooker hoods.

Energy Labeling Extractor Hood

In Figure 13 you can see the energy label for cooker hoods. Here you see the brand or the name of the manufacturer with model name (1), the energy efficiency class (2), the energy consumption in kilowatt hours (kWh) per year (3). Here, the assumption is that the fume extraction is one hour per day and the light is two hours in operation per day. The actual consumption depends on your actual usage. In addition, you can see the air guide efficiency (4), which is also called fluid dynamic efficiency. This is divided into the classes A-G. The same classification A-B also has the grease separation grade (6). Likewise, the lighting efficiency (5) is divided into the classes A-G. The volume (7) is given in decibels (dB). Devices with approx. 70 dB correspond to the volume of a vacuum cleaner. The lower the value, the quieter the device works.

The best energy efficiency class from 2018 on is A +++.

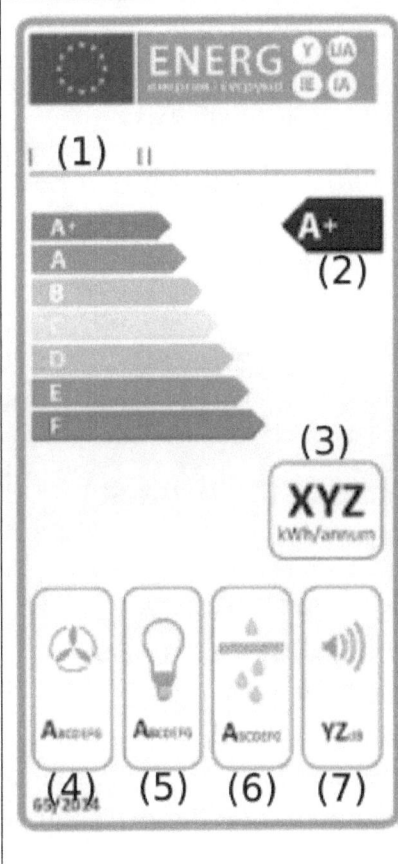

1) Trade mark or name of the manufacturer with model name

2) Energy Efficiency

3) Energy consumption in kilowatt hours (kWh) per year Assumption: operation 1 hour daily and lighting 2 hours daily.)

4) Air conduction efficiency (also called fluid dynamic efficiency) is divided into classes A-G

5) Lighting efficiency, is divided into classes A-G

6) Degreasing

	efficiency is classified into classes A-G
	7) Volume in decibels (dB), highest setting during normal usage.
	Note to the extractor hood:
	The best energy efficiency class has been A +++ since 2018.

Figure 13: Energy consumption marking for the extractor hood.

The water heater

The engineer Hugo Junkers registered in 1894 the patent of a "gas fired oven". On this basis, he founded his company Junkers and Co. one year later. This gas bath furnace was based on the same principle that we still use in our water heaters, except that it was much larger in his time.

Operation principle of the water heater

Electric water heaters are connected to a closed water supply system and heat water with the flow principle. The water is heated at the moment when it is needed in the place where it is needed. It is thus a decentralized system. It does not have a tank, such as a boiler has it. Though, hot water is continuously available. As a result, theoretically both the kitchen and the bathroom can be supplied continuously with hot water. If you are looking for a new device, be aware of the flow rate you need for the device performance.

There are two types of water heaters. The hydraulically controlled water heater and the electronically controlled instantaneous water heater. In both systems, the water is heated by direct contact with the heating coils. This principle is called bare-wire heating system. This principle has the advantage that the heating coils do not calcify, since these are directly in the water and the lime does not adhere permanently due to the flow of water. As a result, the heating block is maintenance-free and you usually have no costs and efforts.

It should nevertheless be considered that after working on the water system, the device must be free of air, otherwise the heating coils can be destroyed.

The *hydraulically* controlled water heater regulates the heating power via the water pressure and the flow rate. The disadvantage here is that it can lead to temperature differences when there are pressure fluctuations. The typical example here is that the water may suddenly become cold during a shower because someone else for example is opening the faucet.

In the case of an *electronic* water heater, the temperature in the inlet is measured and, in accordance with the set target value, the heating capacity is regulated above previously defined values.

For *fully electronic* water heaters, the temperature is measured both in the inlet and in the outlet. Thus, a temperature accurate to the exact degree can be controlled by the electronics.

Disadvantages of electronic water heaters are above all the very high electricity costs. With uncontrolled water heaters, a constant temperature can not be achieved, which is negative for the well-being. When hot and cold water comes in turns, everyone jumps and no one is happy. Until the water is heated, a few liters of water are needed or to be precise wasted.

In contrast to gas water heaters, primary energy is used in electric instantaneous water heaters, since the transformation from coal to electricity causes losses and, in addition, losses occur during the transport of the electricity. A rule of thumb says that transforming and transporting the electricity per 100 km causes a loss of 1%. In 2008 there was a total loss of 6.4% in Germany.[19]. That means, on average, there was a distance of 640 km between the generator of electricity and the consumer. In 2012, this value dropped to 510 km.

The use of a more favorable night stream is not possible with an electric water heater, as the electricity or the heated water is not stored.

---

19 [16] (Proteus)

The advantages of electronic water heaters are the compact design, the existing ECO programs and the children or scalding protection. They are easy to install and the cables to be laid are usually short, which means less heat loss. Since there is no storage such as the boiler, there is no heat loss either. In addition, there is no risk with bacteria that can multiply in water reservoirs. The water is heated only when it is needed and the hot water is thus limitless available.

Comparison with other systems

Electronic water heaters, unlike the hydraulic system, do not require the addition of cold water. This can save up to 20% in energy.

If you have a gas connection, then a gas water heater is preferable because of the lower running costs.

If you have a heat pump or a photovoltaic system, an electric water heater is to be preferred, as this allows you to use your produced electricity directly on site. In addition, the self-produced electricity is cheaper despite the installation and maintenance costs.

Electronic water heater	
Advantages	**Disadvantages**
Compact design.	Very high electricity costs.
Easy to install.	For uncontrolled instantaneous water heaters, no constant temperature.
Efficient in the use of electricity.	Until water is heated, a few liters of water are wasted.
Child or scald protection.	High primary energy consumption compared to gas water heaters.
ECO programs available.	No use of night-electricity possible.
No heat loss through a storage tank (boiler).	
Low heat loss through lines, as usually close to the point of	

consumption.	
Unlimited hot water supply.	
No bacteria problem, as no stagnant water.	

Table 18: Advantages and disadvantages of an electronic water heater.

Electronic water heater
compared to
Electronic instantaneous water heaters, unlike the hydraulic system, do not require the addition of cold water. This can save up to 20% in energy.
If there is a gas connection, then a gas water heater is preferable because of lower running costs.
If a heat pump or photovoltaic system is available, then an electric instantaneous water

heater is to be preferred, as the direct use of the produced electricity is possible.

Table 19: Electronic instantaneous water heater: comparisons.

Size of an electric instantaneous water heater:

Small storage (about 3-10 kW) are suitable for the kitchen and the toilet.

Small instantaneous water heaters (about 10-18 kW) are suitable for the kitchen and the bathroom for a 1- to 2-person household.

Large instantaneous water heaters (about 18-27 kW) are suitable for the bathroom for a 3- to 4-person household.

Functional principle of a fully electronic instantaneous water heaters

When you turn on the tap, the water begins to flow. The following descriptions can be seen in 14.

In the cold water inlet (1), the temperature is measured via a sensor (2) and sent to the control electronics. If a water flow is registered at the flow sensor (3), the process-controlled engine valve (4) and the heating block (5) are controlled via it. The motor valve regulates the flow rate, which allows the device to set the temperature to the nearest degree. At the outlet sensor (6), the temperature of the heated water is measured and the water can be used (7).
Depending on how much water comes (flow rate) more or less heating coils in the heating block (5) are turned on. The water is heated in the heating block (5) in direct contact with the heating coils, which is the most efficient energy transfer.

When you close the tap, the pressure in the pipe breaks down and the circuit in the heating block is interrupted. If this does not happen, a safety mechanism is installed. This is followed by a check valve and an overpressure is created. This overpressure moves a membrane of the safety switch and interrupts the power supply to the heating coils. Such a safety mechanism should be present in every water heater for your own safety.

Simple models of a water heaters usually have an analog knob to adjust the temperatures. With a 3-stage adjustable device, it is only possible to decide between the fixed preset temperatures. Most are 35°C, 45°C and 55°C. This is sufficient for the shower and the sink. If you want to set a different temperature, then cold water is added. If you want, for example, 50°C, the water is still heated to 55°C and mixed with cold water. This is not efficient in terms of energy and you can pay for this 5°C more. Therefore, it makes more sense to buy a continuously adjustable water heater. These can usually be adjusted to 0.5°C "exactly to the wanted degree".

For those who wants to adjust the temperature conveniently by remote control, because it is more pleasant or because the device was installed in a place that is difficult to reach, there are also alternatives. In addition to a remote control also water heaters controlled via Wi-Fi and an application are available. For these, however, you have to pay more.

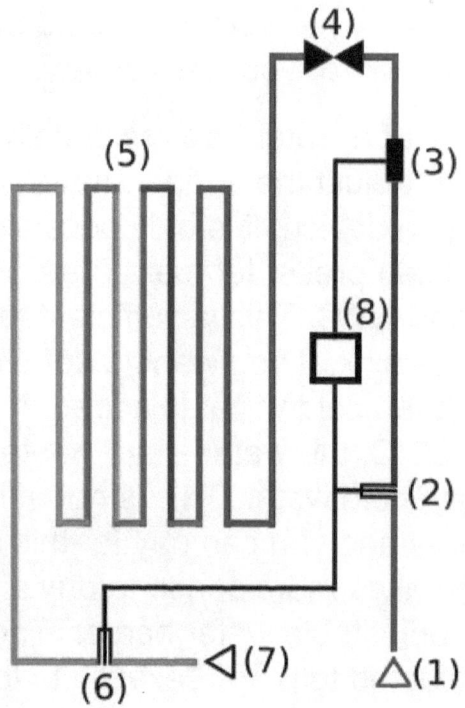

Figure 14: Operating principle of a continuous water heater. 1) inlet cold water, 2) temperature sensor inlet, 3) flow sensor, 4) valve, 5) heating block, 6) temperature sensor outlet, 7) hot water outlet, 8) control electronics;

Decision-making opportunities and summary for the instantaneous water heater

If you want to buy a new instantaneous water heater, you can choose between an electronic controlled or a full electronic controlled instantaneous water heater, a hydraulically controlled instantaneous water heater or a gas powered instantaneous water heater.

Electronic vs. hydraulic instantaneous water heater	
Electronic	**Hydraulic**
Closed water heater.	Closed water heater.
Infinitely adjustable..	Gradually adjustable.
Better efficiency.	Lower efficiency.
Precise temperature.	Temperature fluctuations has to be expected.
No minimum flow.	Minimum flow required.
Higher acquisition costs.	Lower acquisition costs.
Lower running costs.	Higher running costs.
All-purpose water heater.	Only recommended for kitchen and guest toilet (if any).

Table 20: Comparison of electronic and hydraulic instantaneous water heaters.

The device should be placed as close to the consumer as possible to keep the water pipes as short as possible. The longer the lines are, the higher the heat losses. You have the choice between a wall and a saucer mounting.

In addition, a distinction is made between an open (unpressurised) and a closed (pressure-resistant) system.

In an open device, the system is not under water pipe pressure, also called pressureless system, and it can also be used only a single tap, such as a single sink. It is important to note that special fittings are required, for example standard fittings must not be used. If a fitting has three connection pipes, you can use them for this. In this case, the container is always connected to the outside air. When the hot water tap is opened, the cold water inlet is opened and the cold water pushes the lighter upper water upwards towards the faucet.

In a closed device, the system is under water line pressure (usually about 6 bar), also called pressure-resistant system and it can be used several taps, such as a bathroom, a sink and a shower. In the closed system, all commercially available pressure fittings can be used.

With instantaneous water heaters, there are numerous equipment from which you can choose and decide for yourself. Among other things, they have a memory function and a display.

For additional convenience, some manufacturers offer remote controls. These are handy when the device is in a hard place to reach .

Further comfort features are WLAN-enabled or per app controllable instantaneous water heaters. There you can easily make all sorts of settings from your smartphone, tablet or PC and view the consumption data from your sofa. A practical way to save energy is also that you can set and save your personal temperatures and energy saving functions there.

In addition, there are some safety features that should be considered. In addition to a safety shutdown and a frost protection circuit, there are also child safety devices, indicator lights, bubble control sensors, temperature warning indicators, splash water protection, jet water protection, temperature limiter, scalding hazard indicator, scald protection and overheating protection. Inform yourself when buying it, to protect your loved ones and yourself.

Please also note whether your device is suitable for plastic pipes if you want to use one.

A timer helps you to adjust the temperature according to time and save energy.

If you own or want to install a solar panel system, remember that your instantaneous water heater should also be suitable for solar use.

Often when buying a useful mounting template is included. This helps you with the self-assembly of the device.

To choose the right performance, you can use the following examples. For bathtub, shower and sink you need about 18 kW, if you only want to operate a sink, 10 kW are enough. Small instantaneous water heaters can heat up to approx. 35°C. By contrast, large instantaneous water heaters can heat up to approx. 60°C. But temperatures of up to 85°C are also possible.

With strongly calcareous water, the water heater is better suited to a boiler, since only the water needed has to be heated to the actual temperatures and in a bare wire heating, the heating wires are in direct contact with the water and thereby solves and cleans the lime scale again and again by itself.

Water heater	
Decision-making possibilities	**Support for your decision-making**
Product type Temperature control	Electronically regulated Electronically controlled Hydraulically regulated Hydraulically controlled Gas water heater
Assembly	Under-counter mounting Wall mounting
Design type	Closed system (with pressure) Open system (without pressure)
Options	Memory function Display Remote control W-Lan or App-enabled Frost protection circuit

	Child lock
	Indicator light
	Suitable for plastic pipe
	Bubble detection
	Solar panel suitable
	Temperature warning indicators
	Mounting template
	Timer
	Safety shutdown
	Splash protection
	Splash water protection
	Temperature
	Danger of scalding display
	Scald protection
	Overheating protection
Power	Only sink (kitchen or guest toilet): about 3-10 kW are sufficient. For bath, shower and washbasin: about 10-18 kW

	are sufficient.. For 3- to 4-person household: about 18-27 kW are sufficient..
Upper temperature limit	Small instantaneous water heaters: maximum approx. 35°C. Medium through-flow heaters: approx. 35°C-60°C. Large instantaneous water heaters: approx. 60°C - up to 85°C possible.
Temperature levels	From one level to five levels possible. Infinity control.
Heating system	Bare wire: Clarification needed before buying, if a power connection is needed. Gas: Clarification necessary if a gas connection is available.
Operating voltage	230V

	400V
Water quality	Low-lime water
	Lime-rich water
	Or suitable for both
Volume	15 dB (normal, very quiet, quieter than a tick of a wristwatch)
Annual electricity consumption (2 persons, 2 hours per week average, 30.5 cents / kWh with 25 kWh water heater).	About 779 €
Energy efficiency class	A+
	A
	B
	C
	D
	E
	F
Acquisition cost	From about 55 € to over 1,600 € possible.

Savings potential with new purchase	80 € saving potential per year, if, for example, instead of 25 kW device, a 18 kW device can be used.

Table 21: Decision-making possibilities and support for your decision-making for the instantaneous water heater.

Attention: If you have installed and connected the water heater, allow water to flow into the unit before switching it on.

Saving tips instantaneous water heater

The first saving method for the instantaneous water heater, which you spontaneously think about, is certainly the device itself, to lower the temperature. A temperature of just under 40°C are usually sufficient for the shower. For the kitchen sink about 45°C are sufficient. You should only go over that if you really can not live without even hotter water. If you do not have to readjust in the shower when the hot water tap is fully open, the appliance is set correctly. Otherwise you have to mix cold water with the already heated water. Test out how many degrees Celsius you can downgrade.

If you do not need hot water, or if you only need water for a short time, and you only turn the tap on for a few seconds, set the faucet completely to the cold water position. Otherwise, the instantaneous water heater will start, but you will not notice the heated water as it will take some time for the water to heat up first, and second, until it reaches you. On the way to you, the pipes must first be heated.

Water heater	
Saving possibilities	**Support for your decision-making**
Reducing flow rate	Do not turn on the faucet completely (flow reduction).
Descaling	Regular descaling guarantees the highest possible efficiency of the heating coil. Not necessary with bare wire heating.
Reducing temperature	Set the temperature as high as necessary, but as low as possible.
Water tap	If hot water is not needed, or if you only need water for a short time, turn the faucet completely to the cold position.
Saving potential	About 20 € saving potential per year.

Table 22: Savings possibilities and support for your decision-7 for instantaneous water heaters.

Energy Label Water Heater

Figure 15 shows the energy labeling for instantaneous water heaters. Here you can see the trade mark or the name of the manufacturer with model name (1) and the hot water preparation function and the load profile (2). The faucet symbol represents the hot water preparation function. The letter behind it represents the load profile. Table 23 shows an overview of the possible load profiles. In addition, you can see the energy efficiency (3), divided into classes A+ to F. Here it is assumed that the instantaneous water heater is put into operation 365 days a year as follows.

From 00:00 to 06:59 o'clock there is no hot water withdrawal.

From 07:00 to 23:59 o'clock, depending on the tap profile, a hot water withdrawal takes place.

Depending on whether it is an individual or a family, a corresponding amount or duration is calculated accordingly for showers, cleaning, rinsing, etc.

The actual consumption depends on your actual usage. In addition, you can see the energy consumption per year in kWh (4). The volume (5) is represented by the house symbol and the loudspeaker symbol and is expressed in decibels (dB). As a rule, these work very quietly, about 15 dB. By contrast, water heaters with a heat pump are louder. Here you should check the volume in any case. In addition, a symbol is indicated below that stands for the low load periods (6), that is to say for the low-cost tariffs. The best energy efficiency class has been A+ since October 2017.

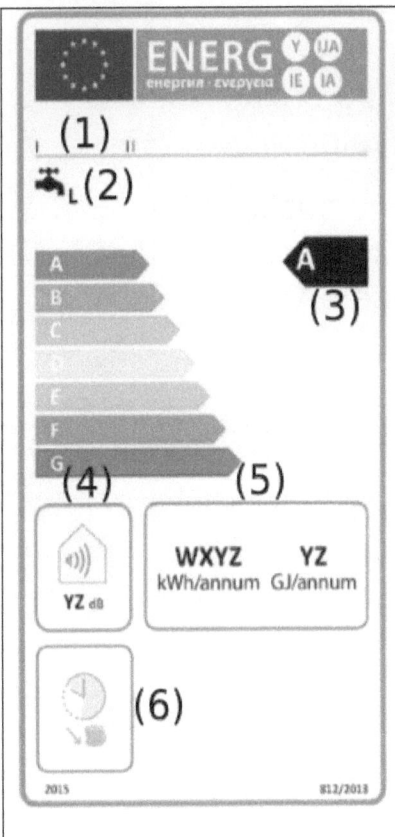

1) Trade mark or name of the manufacturer with model name.

2) Hot water preparation functions and load profile: The tap symbol represents the water heating function. The letter behind it shows the load profile. Table 23 shows an overview of the possible load profiles.

3) Energy efficiency (divided into classes A+ to F).

4) Volume in decibels

	(dB). 5) Energy consumption per year in kWh or in GJ. 6) Low load times (low-cost tariffs). Note on the water heater: The best energy efficiency class has been A+ since October 2017.

Figure 15: Energy label for the instantaneous water heater.

Further links for details:

Commission Delegated Regulation (EU) No 812/2013:
http://eur-lex.europa.eu/legal-content/DE/TXT/PDF/?uri=CELEX:32013R0812&from=DE

Commission Regulation (EU) No 814/2013:
http://eur-lex.europa.eu/legal-content/DE/TXT/PDF/?uri=CELEX:32013R0814&from=DE

Directive 2009/125 / EC of the European Parliament and of the Council:
http://eur-lex.europa.eu/legal-content/DE/TXT/PDF/?uri=CELEX:32009L0125&from=DE

Water heater	
oad profile	**Operation area**
3XS	A small sink with a maximum of 35°C.
XXS	A sink with maximum 35°C.
XS	A single shower.
S	A shower and a sink with maximum 35°C
M	Several showers and sink with maximum 55°C.
L	Bath, shower and sink with maximum 35°C.
XL	Several bathrooms with bath, shower and sink with maximum 55°C.
XXL	Several bathrooms with simultaneous use.
3XL	Complete supply of a small apartment building (about 15 people).
4XL	Complete supply of a large apartment building (about 25 people).

Table 23: Load profiles and their applications for the instantaneous water heater.

The load profiles show you the location or intended use of the instantaneous water heater.

The load profiles 3XS and XXS are suitable for a small sink, for example in a guest toilet.

The load profiles XS and S are suitable for a shower alone. At S, even a small sink can be switched to.

The load profiles M, L and XL are devices that are suitable for several showers and sinks.

The load profiles XXL, 3XL and 4XL are intended for the supply of large houses with several bathrooms, or for the supply of an apartment building.

The stand-by operation

The stand-by mode runs in the background and unnoticed by many users. Electricity consumption is underestimated by most, but accounts for approximately 10% of the total household budget. It seems that the device is turned off, but most devices continue to work in the background. Of course, it consumes less energy than when it's on, but since it happens 24 hours a day, seven days a week, and 365 days a year, it adds up to a sizeable sum. These so-called no-load losses are shown here and we try to find ways to eliminate them.

As the Federal Environment Agency has calculated two medium-sized nuclear power plants are needed alone for the no-load losses in Germany. This equates to about 22 billion kWh of electricity or in other words 22000 million kWh20. Figure 16 shows Germany's electricity consumption by sector from 1990 to 2016. The top green bars correspond to the households, including the light blue bars of the industry next to the top bars, including the yellow bars of the trade, commerce and services and the lowest dark blue bars to the traffic. 2009 is due to the global economic crisis a drop can be seen. Electricity consumption rose continuously before that. However,

20 [17] [UBA]

after 2010, the new rules on energy transition came into force, you can see a reduction. A confirmation that even you can save a lot of money with energy-efficient appliances and savings tips, as the decline is mainly attributable to households. Electricity consumption in the industry remained roughly the same, despite years of economic growth.

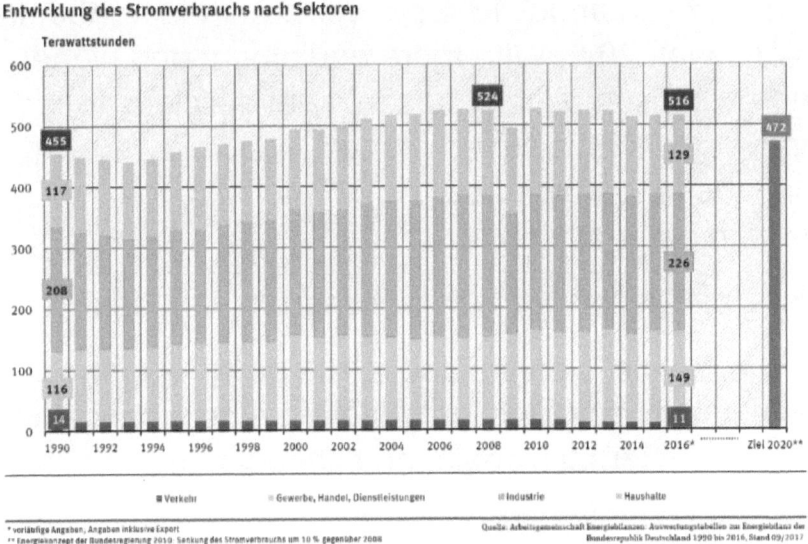

Figure 16: The power consumption of Germany from 1990 to 2016 [UBA].

According to the EU regulation, from 2010 new appliances can consume a maximum of one watt and from 2014 a maximum of 0.5 watt [UBA]. This is a very good step in the right direction. Even if it seems that the consumer (and you too) has nothing to do here, it is still only apparent. If a household has the latest equipment, which consumes only 0.5 watts and we assume there are only ten devices (there are up to 30 electrical appliances in the home and over 100 are theoretically possible appliances) in standby mode, then with a price of 30.5 cents per kWh it would cost you about 13 € per year. For older models with one watt 26 €. With more equipment and higher stand-by consumption, you could eat delicious foods every year with this saved money - and only by saving the stand-by mode. Not to mention you can save with other saving tips.

Here, a distinction is made between four modes[21]:

Off: The device is connected to the power supply, but does not fulfill any function. Also by remote condition, external or internal signals, no change in the operating mode can be achieved.

Stand-by passive: The device is connected to the power supply, but does not fulfill any main functions. However, the device can be switched to another operating mode by remote control or another internal signal.

Stand-by Active: Same functions as Stand-by Passive. In addition, however, the device may be

21 [18] [EU-Modi]

brought into an alternate operating mode with an external signal or information from an external source. Means: always ready to do something.

On: The device is power-connected and performs key functions, but can also provide signals to supported devices.

As a first test, you can feel with your hand whether the device is warm when it is off. If so, then you can assume that cost-relevant electricity is flowing, for which you pay.

To really measure if and how much an electrical appliance consumes power, plug in an ammeter. At consumer centers and environmental organizations, you can borrow a power meter and check your electrical appliances one by one. There are already in the market from about 20 €. It's best to start with the familiar power guzzlers, such as consumer electronics and modem devices.

The future of the kitchen

Next I want to digress a bit and show the fascinating possibilities of the kitchen of the future.

Cooling units with magnetic cooling

The method of magnetic cooling is based on the "magnetocaloric effect" (MCE). This was discovered in 1917 by the physicists P. Weiss and A. Picard. It states that magnetic materials heat up when they are moved into a magnetic field and cool when moving out of a magnetic field.[22] In recent years, progress has been made with non-toxic, common materials at room temperature.

If the magnetocaloric material moves into the magnetic field, it heats up and this heat is dissipated. The material is near room temperature. If the magnetocaloric material moves out of the magnetic field again, it cools down and can absorb heat, for example from the refrigerator, whereby the refrigerator cools down. This process is repeated again and again.

Among other things, General Electric researched this system. They say that this new principle should be

22 [20]

20% more efficient than conventional cooling technology, without toxic substances and chemicals[23]. This considerably simplifies the recycling of old refrigerators. A few years ago, General Electric sold this division"GE Appliance". Unfortunately I could not get an answer to the progress of this project on several requests. Therefore, it is time to wait and hope that this technology will soon be ready for the market.

Torsional refrigeration by twisted, coiled, and supercoiled fibers

Twisted nickel-titanium wires is one of the newest researches in the world to cool down the air. Researchers from China, America and Germany are working parallel on this approach.

In the past this method was done by researchers in Texas and they initially pulled out rubber fibers and then twisted them so long until a tangle emerged. When this tension was released, the temperature of the material decreased by 16.4 degrees Celsius. If you do this with twisted nickel-titanium wires the temperature falled down to 20,8 degrees.

Unfortunately this method is in the beginning of the research, but its potential is huge.

---

23 [21]

Intelligent connected network devices

Another field that is being researched is smart appliances and kitchen utensils. Refrigerators will recognize how old and good the food is, what foods have expired and what foods need to be bought. And of course, there will be the possibility that the refrigerator will automatically order the food which went out. For example, Samsung has introduced a smart refrigerator with a large display. On this you can see the contents inside the refrigerator, make notes and order food.[24]

Pots will recognize how many ingredients the vegetables have and adjust the cooking time. Even with ovens, the baking time is adjusted and thus energy can be saved.

And of course: All kitchen appliances communicate with each other and with you.

---

24 [22]

Print food via 3D printer

Another way to prepare food in the future is to simply print it out by using a 3D printer, such as the Procusini 3D printer.[25] It can create 3D shapes that look completely different from how we know it. It is now mainly used for decorative desserts.

Robots

Another possibility is that robots prepare food for us and what most of us will like best: the robot also does the dishes. Such a cooking robot already exists. The team of Moley Robotics has developed it and already controls over 100 recipes and is constantly evolving.[26] The movements of cook Tim Anderson were recorded and transmitted to the robot. It will be interesting to see how the development continues and when we can buy the first robot for our own home.

Free-Range cookers

A free-range cooker is a cooker where you put any pot on the stove surface and at this point it heats up.

---

25   [23]

26   [24]

The surface adapts to the pot and thus you save energy.[27]

---

27 [25]

Summary tables

The following tables provide an overview of the cost and information of the household appliances described in this book. The average electricity costs of 2017 in Germany of 30.5 cents per kWh were used (see also Figure 1).

Table 24 gives an overview of the average power consumption, the average power consumption per year, the average usage time per day of household appliances in the kitchen with energy efficiency class A+ compared to 15 year old appliances. The services are in watt and the power consumption in kWh per year. The last column shows the average usage time per week used for the specific device. This is a logically chosen time for a two person household. However, you will need to adjust this value for yourself because some devices will not be at your household, some devices will rarely be used and other devices will use them more often or mainly. Therefore, you should not simply sum up all the values to find out that the total electricity cost would be much too high. Everyone has their own habits, which of course cannot all be listed here. However, with the tables, you can find clues from which you can rely on yourself.

As an example we look at the fridge. Even if it seems for you to work 24 hours a day, the compressor does not always work. Here I have set a default of 4.8 hours a day, which means someone rarely opens the fridge. However, if you are someone who opens the refrigerator door every 10 minutes, the compressor will try to recover the lost cold and the usage time increases accordingly. Opening the door every time, this increases the consumption by approx. 10%.

Die Küche 2 Personen Haushalt	Durchschnittliche Leistung A+ [Watt]	Durchschnittlicher Stromverbrauch A+ [kWh/Jahr]	15 Jahre alt Leistung [Watt]	15 Jahre alt Stomverbrauch [kWh/Jahr]	Durchschnittliche Verwendungszeit pro Woche
Kühlschrank	130	228	240	420	34 Stunden
Spülmaschine	1600	117	2200	161	84 Minuten
Backofen	3000	274	5000	456	105 Minuten
Backofen mit Umluft	2100	192	5000	456	105 Minuten
Herd	1000	110	1500	164	126 Minuten
Mikrowelle	1000	40	1000	40	45 Minuten
Wasserkocher	2000	17	2000	17	10 Minuten
Toaster	850	7	850	7	10 Minuten
Abzugshaube	100	11	100	11	126 Minuten
Durchlauferhitzer	25000	2555	25000	2800	2,0 Stunden

Table 24: Overview of the average power, the average power consumption per year, the average usage time per week of household appliances in the kitchen with energy efficiency class A+ compared to 15 year old appliances.

In Table 25, in the first column, you can see the share of the total electricity consumption of a household, which I call the "generally accepted values". These are most frequently cited in the literature, with corresponding deviations, of course. In addition, you will find my own calculations, once with an electric water heater and once without an electric water heater.

The most noticeable thing in the first column is the very high proportion of the refrigerator in the household. Whole 17% should make this. If you look at today's refrigerators with an energy efficiency class A+, you can see an average power of about 130 watts. To reach the value of 17%, you would have to open the fridge day and night, put in lots of hot food or have it standing next to the oven. My own calculations come to about 9-10%, which is a more reasonable value for a two-person household. As a result, the values of other household appliances change accordingly.

The other device with a big difference is the oven. This accounts for a total of 11.4% of the total electricity consumption in the household. At 3,000 watts and only 105 minutes usage time a week, you have a consumption of 274 kWh per year. You can pay 83.40 € per year. If you bake only with circulating air, the total power consumption is reduced to 8.0%. Only with this option would you save 25 € per year.

Die Küche 2 Personen Haushalt	Anteil am Gesamtstromverbrauch im Haushalt (Allgemein akzeptierte Werte) [%]	Anteil am Gesamtstromverbrauch im Haushalt Eigene Berechnung Ohne Durchlauferhitzer [%]	Anteil am Gesamtstromverbrauch im Haushalt Eigene Berechnung Mit Durchlauferhitzer [%]
Kühlschrank	17,0	9,5	6,7
Spülmaschine	3,0	4,9	3,4
Backofen	5,0	11,4	8,1
Backofen mit Umluft	5,0	8,0	5,6
Herd	4,0	4,6	3,2
Mikrowelle	0,5	1,7	1,2
Wasserkocher	0,2	0,7	0,5
Toaster	0,5	0,3	0,2
Abzugshaube	1,7	0,5	0,3
Durchlauferhitzer	33	-	75,1

Table 25: Generally accepted and self-calculated proportion of household appliances in the kitchen to the total electricity consumption of a household.

Table 26 gives an overview of the average total cost per year for energy efficiency class A+ compared to a 15 year old equipment. This will serve as a guide to how much the cost should be and how much you could save compared to a 15-year-old device.

You can save a lot in the kitchen with a new fridge, about 59 € per year. With the water heater, the bath was added, resulting in a saving of about 60 € per year. Only for the kitchen, the savings are correspondingly lower. It was assumed that you replace your old hydraulic instantaneous water heater with an electronic instantaneous water heater.

Thereafter, an exchange is most likely to pay off the oven, the dishwasher and the stove. With the dishwasher, the savings potential of water would have to be taken into account, which makes about 850 liters a year compared to a 15-year-old device. This corresponds to about 3 € savings per year. Thus, you would save a total of 14 € a year with a new dishwasher.

With the oven you would save about 56 € per year. If you would use the recirculation function every time, there will be another 25 € savings, which means a total savings of 81 € each year.

Die Küche 2 Personen Haushalt	Durchschnittliche Gesamtkosten pro Jahr A+ [€]	Durchschnittliche Gesamtkosten pro Jahr 15 Jahre alt [€]	Sparpotential pro Jahr [€]	Sparpotential pro Jahr CO2 in kg	Sparpotential pro Jahr CO2 im km Autofahrt
Kühlschrank	69	128	59	154	1018
Spülmaschine	36	49	11 (14)	35	231
Backofen	83	139	56	146	964
Backofen mit Umluft	58	139	81	212	1397
Herd	33	50	17	44	289
Mikrowelle	12	12	0	0	0
Wasserkocher	5	5	0	0	0
Toaster	2	2	6	0	0
Abzugshaube	3	3	0	0	0
Durchlauferhitzer	779	854	75	196	1294

Table 26: Overview of the average total cost per year of household appliances in the kitchen with energy efficiency rating A + compared to 15 year old appliances. In addition the saving potential in euro, in CO2 in kg and in CO2 in km by car.

Overview of all household electrical appliances

In Table 27 you find a list of commonly used equipment in a household. The list contains 97 devices. By definition, obsolete electrical appliances such as electric pencil sharpeners or palmtops have been deliberately left out. Also very rare devices such as electric can opener, crepe device, electric toilet seat or electrical equipment in your own workshop, such as a lathe, are also not included.

The list should show you how many electrical appliances are there and thus how much savings potential there is.

If you take theoretically half of 50 devices and half of which has a stand-by mode of 0.5 watts, you would have thereby already costs of 67 € per year.

This too should give you only a clue and a feeling for what can be saved in your own household.

Kitchen	Household	Entertainment
fridge	night light	HiFi System
dishwasher	Vacuum cleaner	CD player
oven	Hand vacuum cleaner	DVD player
stove	Lighting	language assistants Alexa / Siri
hood	ornamental fountains	alarm clock
water heater	(Emergency) hand lamp	radio
egg cooker	animal equipment (cat gate /aquarium)	television
microwave	washing machine	SAT / DVB Box
coffee machine	dryer	game console

continuous-flow water heater	electric heaters	video camera
freezer	ventilator	Keyboard
toaster	iron	electric railway
fryer	waffle iron	christmas lights
electronic scale	Raclette	security camera
juicer	wine refrigerator	Amplifier / booster
food processor	Mixer / blender	musical instruments
	projector	toys

Home Appliances	Communication / Office	Hygiene Health
automatic garage door	(Wireless) phone	electric toothbrush
heating control	answering machine	razor
motion detector	mobile phone	cross-trainer
boiler / central heating	baby radio monitoring	massage chair
alarm system	modem	hairdryer
mowing machine	computer	winding bar
pond / fountain	screen	towel heater
high pressure cleaner	laptop	
drilling machine	printer	
air conditioning	scanner	**other**

electric heater	speaker	electric bicycle
ventilation equipment	fax machine	electric car
sewing machine	router	power-bank
smoke detector	charger	various watches
fragrant plug	external hard drive	electronic notebooks
heat pumps	CD burner	paper shredder
	calculator	e-book reader

Table 27: Overview of commonly used household appliances that require electrical power. There are 98 devices. No guarantee of completeness.

Attachment

What is energy?

Energy is the ability of a system to do work. It can not be created or destroyed. It can only be transformed from one form of energy to another. For example, energy from altitude energy can be converted into kinetic energy. That is, if you let a stone fall from the bridge (altitude energy), then it falls / moving down (kinetic energy).

The energy is a universal size, means it applies everywhere, without exception.

There are different forms of energy.

The Mechanical energy is the energy contained in bodies that the body receives through its location (altitude energy) or through its motion (kinetic energy).

The electrical energy is the energy that can be transmitted by electricity or stored in electric fields. It has the ability to do mechanical work, to give off heat or to emit light.

The magnetic energy is the energy of a magnetic field.

Chemical energy is the energy that is stored in a chemical compound that can be released through chemical reactions.

Thermal energy is the energy stored in the disordered motion of the atoms or molecules of a substance. The faster the particles move, the hotter the system. If all particles were no longer moving, ie standing still, this would correspond to 0 Kelvin, which corresponds to -273°C (minus 273 degrees Celsius). There is nothing in the universe that is even colder.

Radiation energy is the energy of electromagnetic waves. Depending on frequency and wavelength, these are microwaves, light, X-rays, etc.

Nuclear energy is the energy contained in the atomic nuclei. It is released during the cracking or fusion of atomic nuclei.

The amount of energy becomes Joule (SI unit, international unit of measurement). A joule (= 1 J) is the work done when the force of one Newton (1 N) acts along a one meter (1 m) path. For example, if you raise an object of one Newton by one meter:

$1 J = 1 N \times 1 m = 1 Nm = 1 kg \times m^2/s^2$.

What is energy efficiency?

Energy efficiency is the ratio of how much energy has to be used to operate. For example, if a light bulb can glow for 15 hours with 1 kWh and an LED can glow with 1 kWh for 100 hours, then the LED bulb is more energy efficient.

If everything becomes more energy efficient, it will contribute to the energy transition, protect the environment and protect your purse, as you will need less power at the same time.

What is an energy efficiency table / energy label?

See the corresponding chapters.

Especially in the chapter „The fridge" on page 19 you can find an introducing text.

What is electricity / electrical current?

There are two types of charges, the positive and the negative. If a body has the same number of positive and negative charges, it is neutral. If one of the two charges predominates, the body has attractive or repulsive properties and interacts with other objects.

This basic phenomenon occurring in nature in the form of electric charges and electricity is called electricity.

If the charged particles move in a directionally directed direction, this is called an electric current.

What is a magnetic field?

A magnetic field is the state of the room, for example around a magnet. This field exerts forces on other magnets and materials with magnetic properties.

Two magnets can both attract and repel.

Each magnetic field has a north and a south pole. Never before a magnet with only one pole has been observed.

Magnetic fields also surround each conductor in which an electric current flows.

Epilogue

An individual analysis in the book for each person is not possible. Therefore, consider the calculations and hints given here and use the useful tips that you can use and that suit you.

Not everyone has all the household appliances, everyone uses the devices differently and for different time lengths and each one has a different brand and age.

If you have any comments or constructive criticism, you can always e-mail me.

„Alexander.Marco.Goldmann@gmail.com"

Or you write a comment on my homepage: www.lelg.net.

If you have successfully applied the tips and saved a lot, I would be happy to hear about it.

Happy work and a good and happy time
wishes you

Alexander Goldmann

BONUS PAGES

Awesome beginner checklist to save money quickly

Here is a list to avoid the biggest mistakes in wasting energy and wasting money and to solve them quickly and with the best way (from a few seconds to just a few minutes).

Much of your money is thus saved from waste.

- ☐ Set the temperature of your fridge higher than 6 degrees Celsius.

- ☐ Set the temperature of your freezer lower than 19 degrees Celsius.

- ☐ During work or when no one is at home, switch off the following devices manually, via a power strip or via a timer:

    - o modem

    - o router

    - o game console

    - o Other devices that get warm without being turned on. (Test by hand).

- ☐ In the kettle only bring the required amount of water to boil, not more.

- ☐ Use water saving attachment for sink and shower. (you can buy it from 2 € and pays for itself very quickly, because less hot water has to be produced).

- ☐ Washing machine always fully loaded.

- ☐ Dishwasher always fully loaded.

- ☐ In the oven pre-heating and reheating usually not necessary.

- ☐ Use the same pot and pan sizes depending on the hob.

- ☐ Use energy saving features on all devices.

- ☐ And finally: the last one turns off the light ☺

Bonus tips

More high-cost money wasters:

- ☐ Hot water pipes should be insulated.
- ☐ If the roof is poorly insulated, up to 20% of the heat can be lost there.
- ☐ Old heat pumps are real power-hungry. An exchange can already be worthwhile within a year.
- ☐ Replace old bulbs with halogen bulbs or LEDs.
- ☐ Borrow instead of buying things that are not constantly needed, such as a drill, saw, lawn mower, etc.
- ☐ Public transport instead of car (gas, wear, insurance ...)
- ☐ Cancel unnecessary contracts.
- ☐ Self-cooking instead of restaurant visits.
- ☐ No debts and pay off as soon as possible.

→ Basically, it is important to live consciously and avoid unnecessary things. But do not forget: live consciously with indulgence and comfort.

So I can only wish you much fun with the money you saved of you will save! And do not forget, the money thus saved should not be spent, but be invested smartly. Use the compounding effect to increase your money in the long term.
For more tips see also my homepage www.lelg.net.

Have fun collecting money

wishes you

Alexander Goldmann
Author of the book "How to save more money"

and

from the blog www.lelg.net.

List of Figures

Figure 1: Overview of electricity prices in Europe in cents per kWh, including the share of taxes and duties.[] 12

Figure 2: Basic principle of the functioning of a refrigerator. 35

Figure 3: Current energy efficiency classes by product group. As of January 2018. Thanks goes to HEA. [9] (Conradi, 2018). 42

Figure 4: Energy labeling for refrigerators and freezers...43

Figure 5: Working principle of the dishwasher.........67

Figure 6: Energy label for dishwasher. 70

Figure 7: Working principle of an oven. 90

Figure 8: Energy label for the oven..........................93

Figure 9: How a stove works. 105

Figure 10: How a microwave works........................120

Figure 11: The first patent-pending toaster. 134

Figure 12: A typical construction of a wall box (with power losses) for an extractor hood (1) with a backflow flap (2) (about 25%), a fly screen (3) (5-95%) and an oblique outer grid (4) (about 25%). The blue lines (5) represents the draft. 161

Figure 13: Energy consumption marking for the extractor hood. 168

Figure 14: Operating principle of a continuous water heater.1) inlet cold water, 2) temperature sensor inlet, 3) flow sensor, 4) valve, 5) heating block, 6) temperature sensor outlet, 7) hot water outlet, 8) control electronics; 179

Figure 15: Energy label for the instantaneous water heater. 196

Figure 16: The power consumption of Germany from 1990 to 2016 [UBA]. 201

List of Tables

Table 1: Possibilities and help for your decisions for the fridge. 25

Table 2: Savings options and help for your decision-makings for the refrigerator....................................34

Table 3: Classification of the energy efficiency class by the Energy Efficiency Index (EEI). 45

Table 4: Possibilities and help for your decisions for the dishwasher..58

Table 5: Savings options and support for decision-making for the dishwasher.......................................64

Table 6: Possibilities and support for your decision-making for the oven. 80

Table 7: Savings tips and support for your decision-making for the oven. 88

Table 8: Possibilities for a new stove and support for your decision-making..100

Table 9: Savings options and support for your decision-making for the stove. 104

Table 10: Decision-making possibilities & Support four your decision making – The microwave. 112

Table 11: Saving possibilities and support for your decision-making for the microwave. 117

Table 12: Decision-making possibilities and support for your decision-making for the kettle....................126

Table 13: Saving possibilities and support for your decision-making for the kettle. 130

Table 14: Decision-making possibilities and support for your decision-making for the toaster. 140

Table 15: Advantages and disadvantages of retractable extractor hoods and downdraft systems. 150

Table 16: Decision-making possibilities and support for your decision-making for cooker hoods............159

Table 17: Savings possibilities and support for your decision-making for cooker hoods. 165

Table 18: Advantages and disadvantages of an electronic water heater. 175

Table 19: Electronic instantaneous water heater: comparisons. 176

Table 20: Comparison of electronic and hydraulic instantaneous water heaters...................................181

Table 21: Decision-making possibilities and support for your decision-making for the instantaneous water heater...189

Table 22: Savings possibilities and support for your decision-7 for instantaneous water heaters..........192

Table 23: Load profiles and their applications for the instantaneous water heater. 199

Table 24: Overview of the average power, the average power consumption per year, the average usage time per week of household appliances in the kitchen with energy efficiency class A+ compared to 15 year old appliances..212

Table 25: Generally accepted and self-calculated proportion of household appliances in the kitchen to the total electricity consumption of a household. ...214

Table 26: Overview of the average total cost per year of household appliances in the kitchen with energy efficiency rating A + compared to 15 year old appliances. In addition the saving potential in euro, in CO_2 in kg and in CO_2 in km by car. 215

Table 27: Overview of commonly used household appliances that require electrical power. There are 98 devices. No guarantee of completeness. 221

Imprint

Alexander Goldmann, Bakırköy, Ataköy, 9. Kısım,
A6B blok, 34158 Istanbul.

Bibliography

[1]   https://1-stromvergleich.com, „https://1-
     stromvergleich.com," 2018. [Online]. Available:
     :a href="https://1-
     stromvergleich.com/strompreise-in-
     europa/#strompreise-europa-land">Infografik
     Strompreise in Europa": Strom-Report</a>.

[2]   „Statista," 2018. [Online]. Available:
     https://de.statista.com/statistik/daten/studie/22
     7182/umfrage/temperatur-im-winter-nach-
     bundeslaendern/.

[3]   S. Bundesamt, „Destatis," [Online]. Available:
     https://www.destatis.de.

[4]   CosmosDirekt, „CosmosDirekt,"
     CosmosDirekt, 26 09 2014. [Online].
     Available:
     https://www.cosmosdirekt.de/veroeffentlichung
     en/altersarmut-51390/.

[5]   B. Esche, „WDR," WDR, 27 04 2016. [Online].
     Available:
     https://www1.wdr.de/wissen/mensch/tag-
     gegen-laerm-100.html.

[6]   S. A. Mayer, „Energiespartipps," www.t-
     online.de, 21 06 2018. [Online]. Available:

https://www.t-online.de/heim-garten/haushaltstipps/id_76941740/strom-sparen-bei-kuehlschrank-und-gefrierschrank.html. [Zugriff am 17 01 2019].

[7] www.verbraucherzentrale.de, „Kühlen und Gefrieren," Verbraucherzentrale, 07 11 2016. [Online]. Available: https://www.verbraucherzentrale.de/wissen/umwelt-haushalt/wohnen/kuehlen-und-gefrieren-10573.

[8] Statista, „Temperatur im Winter 2017/2018 nach Bundesländern," de.statista.com, [Online]. Available: https://de.statista.com/statistik/daten/studie/227182/umfrage/temperatur-im-winter-nach-bundeslaendern/.

[9] M. Conradi, „HEA," 11 01 2018. [Online]. Available: https://www.hea.de/presse/aktuelle-hea-uebersicht-zeigt-vielfalt-beim-energielabel.

[10] www.br.de, „www.br.de," Der Bayern 1 Umweltkommissar, 09 01 2019. [Online]. Available: https://www.br.de/radio/bayern1/inhalt/experten-tipps/umweltkommissar/geschirr-spuelmaschine-umwelt-100.html. [Zugriff am

17 01 2019].

[11] www.kueche-co.de, „Planungstipps," Energie sparen in der Küche, [Online]. Available: https://www.kueche-co.de/inspiration/magazin/planungstipps/energie-sparen-in-der-kueche.

[12] www.bader.at, „www.bader.at," Kochen und Grillen, [Online]. Available: https://www.bader.at/shop/product/backofen-99511-000.

[13] http://www.backofen-und-ceranfeld.de, „Backofen & Ceranfeld Infos," [Online]. Available: http://www.backofen-und-ceranfeld.de/backofen-und-ceranfeld-wissen/backofen-vorheizen-stromsparen/. [Zugriff am 17 01 2019].

[14] www.stmuv.bayern.de, „Nachhaltig konsumieren - Wasser und Energie sparen," [Online]. Available: https://www.stmuv.bayern.de/themen/verbraucherinformation/nachhaltig_konsumieren/wasser_und_energie_sparen.htm. [Zugriff am 17 01 2019].

[15] S. -. T. N. M. o. A. History, „americanhistory.si.edu," 18 06 2014. [Online]. Available:

http://americanhistory.si.edu/lighting/c_choice/
choice2a.htm.

[16] T. Zoerner, „Proteus solutions," 25 03 2013.
[Online]. Available: https://proteus-
solutions.de/Proteus-News:Art.955326.asp.
[Zugriff am 17 01 2019].

[17] U. Zehnder, „Schweizerische
Eidgenossenschaft," 12, 15, 2006.

[18] www.umweltbundesamt.de,
„Umweltbundesamt," 17 07 2008. [Online].
Available:
https://www.umweltbundesamt.de/daten/energ
ie/stromverbrauch. [Zugriff am 17 01 2019].

[19] T. Heinz, „www.planet-wissen.de," Geschichte
des Herdes, 23 07 2018. [Online]. Available:
https://www.planet-
wissen.de/gesellschaft/wohnen/kuechen/pwie
geschichtedesherdes100.html. [Zugriff am 21
01 2019].

[20] www.magnetokalorik.de,
„www.magnetokalorik.de," [Online]. Available:
https://www.magnetokalorik.de/magnetokaloris
cher-prozess.html. [Zugriff am 22 01 2019].

[21] T. Kellner, „GE reports," General Electric, 07
02 2014. [Online]. Available:
https://www.ge.com/reports/post/75911607449

/not-your-average-fridge-magnet/. [Zugriff am 22 01 2019].

[22] C. Laude, „www.onlinehaendler-news.de," 06 01 2016. [Online]. Available: https://www.onlinehaendler-news.de/online-handel/haendler/22177-online-lebensmittelkauf-samsung-kuehlschrank. [Zugriff am 23 01 2019].

[23] www.procusini.com, www.procusini.com, [Online]. Available: https://www.procusini.com/3dfoodprinter-procusini-3-0/. [Zugriff am 23 01 2019].

[24] www.heute.at, „Küche der Zukunft," www.heute.at, 02 04 2018. [Online]. Available: https://www.heute.at/digital/multimedia/story/D ieser-Roboter-kocht-wie-ein-Sternekoch-40193547. [Zugriff am 23 01 2019].

[25] C. B. TV, „Panasonic: Die Küche der Zukunft auf der IFA," Computer Bild TV, 04 09 2017. [Online]. Available: https://www.youtube.com/watch?v=OHLdyRI7 usU. [Zugriff am 23 01 2019].

[26] www.abendblatt.de, „www.abendblatt.de," 08 12 2015. [Online]. Available: https://www.abendblatt.de/ratgeber/wohnen/ar ticle206801231/Energie-sparen-im-Advent-

Tipps-rund-um-den-Ofen.html. [Zugriff am 27 01 2019].

[27] https://www.youtube.com/redirect?event=vide o_description&v=0kwODoxy3zw&redir_token= dhv-UU47TpFRj5UHFAD-c-rN3_F8MTU1MDY3NzQzMEAxNTUwNTkxMD Mw&q=http%3A%2F%2Fwww.miele.de%2Fha ushalt%2Feinbau-geschirrspueler-1532.htm, „Energieeinsparung im neuen Miele Geschirrspüler G6000 I Miele," Miele, 08 04 2016. [Online]. Available: https://www.youtube.com/watch?v=0kwODoxy 3zw. [Zugriff am 19 02 2019].

www.ingramcontent.com/pod-product-compliance
Lightning Source LLC
Chambersburg PA
CBHW030617220526
45463CB00004B/1325